Grade 3

CALIFORNIA
Test Practice

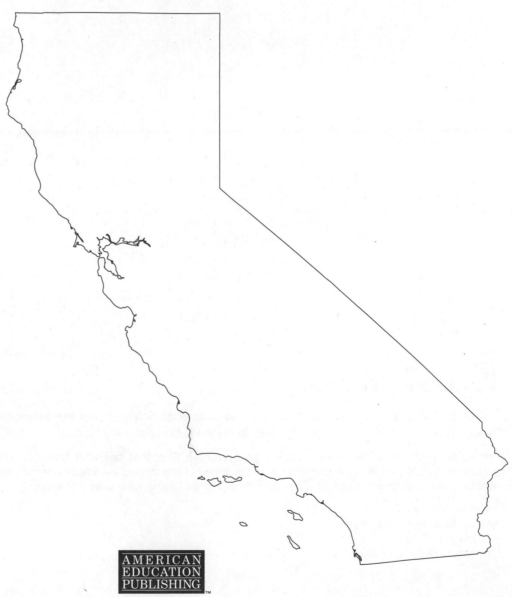

AMERICAN
EDUCATION
PUBLISHING™

Columbus, Ohio

Copyright © 2004 School Specialty Children's Publishing. Published by American Education Publishing™, an imprint of School Specialty Children's Publishing, a member of the School Specialty Family.

Send all inquiries to:
School Specialty Children's Publishing
8720 Orion Place
Columbus, OH 43240-2111

ISBN 0-7696-3033-2

4 5 6 7 8 9 10 PHXBK 09 08 07 06 05 04

Table of Contents

Mathematics

What's Inside?

This workbook is designed to help you and your third-grader understand what he or she will be expected to know on the California third-grade state tests.

Practice Pages

The workbook is divided into a Language Arts section and Mathematics section. Each section has practice activities that have questions similar to those that will appear on the state tests. Students should use a pencil to fill in the correct answers and to complete any writing on these activities.

California Content Standards

Before each practice section is a list of the state standards covered by that section. The shaded "What it means" sections will help to explain any information in the standards that might be unfamiliar.

Mini-Tests and Final Tests

Practice activities are grouped by state standard. When each group of activities is completed, the student can move on to a *Mini-Test* that covers the material presented in those practice activities. After an entire set of standards and accompanying activities are completed, the student should take the *Final Tests*, which incorporate materials from all the practice activities in that section.

Final Test Answer Sheet

The Final Tests have a separate answer sheet that mimics the style of the answer sheet students will use on the state tests. The answer sheet appears at the end of each Final Test.

How Am I Doing?

The *How Am I Doing?* pages are designed to help students identify areas where they are proficient and areas where they still need more practice. Students can keep track of each of their Mini-Test scores on these pages.

Answer Key

Answers to all the practice activities, mini-tests, and final tests are listed by page number and appear at the end of the book.

Frequently Asked Questions

What is STAR?

STAR stands for **S**tandardized **T**esting **A**nd **R**eporting program. It is the name used for the series of tests given to students in California schools.

What kinds of information does my student have to know to pass the test?

The California Department of Education has created a set of guidelines that lists specific skills and information that students must know before moving on to the next grade. Each of these content standards, or learning outcomes, is listed in this workbook and clearly explained. Practice activities have been designed to test your third-grader's mastery of each California content standard.

Are there special strategies or tips that will help my student do well?

The workbook provides sample questions that have content similar to that on the **STAR** tests. Test-taking tips are offered throughout the book.

How do I know what areas my student needs help in?

A special *How Am I Doing?* section will help you and your third-grader evaluate progress. It pinpoints areas where more work is needed, as well as areas where your student excels.

California English-Language Arts Content Standards

The English-language arts content standards developed by the California State Board of Education are divided into four major sections. The information within those sections tells specifically what your third-grader should know or be able to do.

1) Reading

1.0: Word Analysis, Fluency, and Systematic Vocabulary Development

2.0: Reading Comprehension

3.0: Literary Response and Analysis

2) Writing

1.0: Writing Strategies

2.0: Writing Applications (Genres and Their Characteristics)

3) Written and Oral English Language Conventions

1.0: Written and Oral English Language Conventions

4) Listening and Speaking

1.0: Listening and Speaking Strategies

2.0: Speaking Applications (Genres and Their Characteristics)

Language Arts Table of Contents

Reading Standards

1.0 Word Analysis, Fluency, and Systematic Vocabulary Development

Students understand the basic features of reading. They select letter patterns and know how to translate them into spoken language by using phonics, syllabication, and word parts. They apply this knowledge to achieve fluent oral and silent reading.

Decoding and Word Recognition

1.1 Know and use complex word families when reading (e.g., *-ight*) to decode unfamiliar words. *(See page 8.)*

1.2 Decode regular multisyllabic words. *(See page 9.)*

1.3 Read aloud narrative and expository text fluently and accurately and with appropriate pacing, intonation, and expression.

What it means:

Decoding and Word Recognition

- If words are not familiar, students should be able to use letter sounds, syllables, and letter groupings to help them say the words correctly.
- When reading silently or aloud, students should be able to read smoothly, say words correctly, and insert expression where it is appropriate.

Vocabulary and Concept Development

1.4 Use knowledge of antonyms, synonyms, homophones, and homographs to determine the meanings of words. *(See page 10.)*

1.5 Demonstrate knowledge of levels of specificity among grade-appropriate words and explain the importance of these relations (e.g., *dog/ mammal/ animal/ living things*). *(See page 11.)*

1.6 Use sentence and word context to find the meaning of unknown words. *(See page 12.)*

1.7 Use a dictionary to learn the meaning and other features of unknown words. *(See page 13.)*

1.8 Use knowledge of prefixes (e.g., *un-, re-, pre-, bi-, mis-, dis-*) and suffixes (e.g., *-er, -est, -ful*) to determine the meaning of words. *(See page 14.)*

What it means:

Vocabulary and Concept Development

- Students should be able to use several different strategies to help them determine the meaning of unfamiliar words. One important strategy is being able to recognize antonyms, synonyms, homophones, and homographs.
- Students should be able to identify how some words are more specific than others, recognizing, for example, that the word "animal" is a broader term than the word "mammal" and so forth.
- Students should be able to look at familiar words in a sentence or a passage to help them find the meaning of unknown words.
- Students should know how to use a dictionary to look up words and know that the dictionary provides other information about words besides definitions.
- Students should recognize the meaning of common word beginnings, or prefixes, such as *un-, re-,* and *pre-,* and suffixes, such as *-er, -est,* and *-ful*. They can use this knowledge to determine the meaning of unknown words.

Word Families

Example:

Find the word in which the underlined letters have the same sound as the picture name.

- (A) **br**ead
- (B) **bl**ack
- (C) **b**owl
- (D) **b**uy

Answer: (A)

Clue   Repeat the directions to yourself as you look at the answer choices.

1. Find the word that has the same beginning sound as

- (A) **fr**ame
- (B) **fl**ame
- (C) **f**ork
- (D) **f**arm

2. Find the word that has the same ending sound as

- (F) mea**nt**
- (G) sta**nd**
- (H) ea**rn**
- (J) ba**rn**

3. Look at the first word. Find the other word that has the same vowel sound as the underlined part.

fl__oa__t

- (A) block
- (B) board
- (C) chose
- (D) pool

4. Look at the underlined word. Find a word that can be added to the underlined word to make a compound word.

door

- (F) knock
- (G) open
- (H) window
- (J) step

STOP

Reading

1.2

Multi-Syllable Words

Example:

Choose the word that fits into the sentence and is spelled correctly.

A She is not _____ to go.

- (A) eble
- (B) able
- (C) abel
- (D) abell

Answer: (B)

Choose the word that is spelled incorrectly. If all of the words are spelled correctly, choose "No mistakes."

- (F) attack
- (G) funnel
- (H) cousin
- (J) No mistakes

Answer: (J)

DIRECTIONS: Choose the word that fits into the sentence and is spelled correctly.

1. Please don't _____ your new shirt.
- (A) winkle
- (B) wrinkle
- (C) wrinkel
- (D) wrinekle

2. The _____ is surrounded with flowers.
- (F) fountin
- (G) fontain
- (H) fountein
- (J) fountain

3. Jane treated her book _____.
- (A) carlessly
- (B) carelessly
- (C) carelesly
- (D) carelissly

DIRECTIONS: Choose the word that is spelled incorrectly.

4.
- (F) copper
- (G) relaxing
- (H) bandege
- (J) No mistakes

5.
- (A) foraign
- (B) perfume
- (C) tablet
- (D) No mistakes

6.
- (F) sunrise
- (G) shephard
- (H) furniture
- (J) No mistakes

STOP

Reading

1.4

Synonyms and Antonyms

The Great Ice Age

Long ago, the climate of Earth began to cool. As the temperature dropped, giant sheets of ice, called glaciers, moved across the land. As time went on, snow and ice covered many forests and grasslands.

Some plants and animals could not survive the changes in the climate. Other animals moved to warmer land. But some animals were able to adapt. They learned to live with the cold and snowy weather.

Finally, Earth's temperature began to rise. The ice and snow began to melt. Today, the land at the North and South Poles is a reminder of the Great Ice Age.

DIRECTIONS: For each pair of words or phrases, put an **S** if they are synonyms and an **A** if they are antonyms.

1. _____ melt   freeze

2. _____ climate   weather

3. _____ adapt   learn to live with

4. _____ giant sheet of ice glacier

5. _____ rise   fall

6. _____ survive   die

7. _____ warm   cool

8. _____ giant   huge

9. _____ dropped   fell

10. _____ grasslands   prairie

11. _____ remind   forget

12. _____ temperature   measure of heat or cold

Reading

| 1.5 |

Categorizing

Example:

Which of these is a main heading that includes the other three words?

- (A) football
- (B) tennis
- (C) snowboarding
- (D) sports

Answer: (D)

Clue Your first answer choice is probably correct. Don't change it unless you are sure another answer is better.

DIRECTIONS: Choose the heading that includes the other three words.

1.
- (A) fish
- (B) pets
- (C) cats
- (D) birds

2.
- (F) flowers
- (G) rose
- (H) daisy
- (J) tulip

3.
- (A) plate
- (B) cup
- (C) saucer
- (D) dishes

DIRECTIONS: Choose the best answer.

4. **Which book do you think would have the most information about dogs?**
- (F) *The World of Mammals*
- (G) *Animals that Live in the United States*
- (H) *How to Choose a Dog for a Pet*
- (J) *Working Animals*

5. **Which heading in an encyclopedia would give you the most information about Iceland's climate?**
- (A) climate
- (B) Iceland
- (C) geography
- (D) snow

STOP

Reading

1.6

Defining Words in Context

A Boomerang

Have you ever thrown a boomerang to see if it would spin back to you?

Boomerangs are <u>flat, curved objects that can be thrown</u> for fun or as a sport. There are two kinds of boomerangs—returning and nonreturning. A returning boomerang is made to <u>spin through the air in a curve and return</u> to the thrower. It is used mostly for fun or as a sport. The cave dwellers made nonreturning boomerangs. These boomerangs were thrown in a straight path. They were valuable hunting weapons because they could spin through the air and hit a target with great force.

Boomerangs were considered so important that they were often <u>decorated and used in ceremonies.</u>

DIRECTIONS: Look at the underlined phrases in the passage. Decide what is being described by the phrase by looking at the words around it.

1. To what does <u>flat, curved objects that can be thrown</u> refer?

   (A) cave dwellers

   (B) scientists

   (C) boomerangs

   (D) sport

2. To what does <u>spin through the air in a curve and return</u> refer?

   (F) fun or sport

   (G) straight path

   (H) nonreturning boomerang

   (J) returning boomerang

3. To what does <u>decorated and used in ceremonies</u> refer?

   (A) boomerangs

   (B) important

   (C) stick

   (D) stone

STOP

Name _____ Date _____

Using a Dictionary

Clue   Remember, dictionary entries can tell you more than just the meaning of a word. They also can help you say a word correctly and tell you if a word is a noun, verb, adjective, adverb, or pronoun.

DIRECTIONS: Use the dictionary entries to answer numbers 1–3.

save [sāv] *v.* **1.** to rescue from harm or danger. **2.** to keep in a safe condition. **3.** to set aside for future use; store. **4.** to avoid.

saving [sā´vĭng] *n.* **1.** rescuing from harm or danger. **2.** avoiding excess spending; economy. **3.** something saved.

savory [sā´və-rē] *adj.* **1.** appealing to the taste or smell. **2.** salty to the taste.

1. **The *a* in the word *saving* sounds most like the word _____.**
   - (A) pat
   - (B) ape
   - (C) heated
   - (D) naughty

2. **Which sentence uses *save* in the same way as definition number 3?**
   - (F) Firefighters save lives.
   - (G) She saves half of all she earns.
   - (H) Going by jet saves eight hours of driving.
   - (J) The life jacket saved the boy from drowning.

3. **Which sentence uses *savory* in the same way as definition number 2?**
   - (A) The savory stew made me thirsty.
   - (B) The savory bank opened an account.
   - (C) This flower has a savory scent.
   - (D) The savory dog rescued me.

DIRECTIONS: Use the dictionary entry to answer numbers 4 and 5.

beam [bēm] *n.* **1.** a squared-off log used to support a building. **2.** a ray of light. **3.** the wooden roller in a loom. *v.* **1.** to shine. **2.** to smile broadly.

4. **Which use of the word *beam* is a verb?**
   - (F) The beam held up the plaster ceiling.
   - (G) The beam of sunlight warmed the room.
   - (H) She moved the beam before she added a row of wool.
   - (J) The bright stars beam in the night sky.

5. **Which sentence uses the word *beam* in the same way as the first definition of the noun?**
   - (A) The ceiling beam had fallen into the room.
   - (B) The beam of the loom was broken.
   - (C) She beamed her approval.
   - (D) The beam of sunlight came through the tree.

Suffixes and Prefixes

Example:

Find the word in which only the prefix is underlined.

- (A) <u>pre</u>view
- (B) <u>de</u>cide
- (C) <u>al</u>ert
- (D) mon<u>ster</u>

Answer: (A)

1. Find the word in which only the suffix is underlined.
   - (A) bun<u>dle</u>
   - (B) mo<u>stly</u>
   - (C) run<u>ner</u>
   - (D) jump<u>ing</u>

2. Find the word in which only the prefix is underlined.
   - (F) <u>pre</u>tend
   - (G) <u>al</u>low
   - (H) <u>be</u>tween
   - (J) <u>un</u>known

3. Find the word in which only the suffix is underlined.
   - (A) land<u>ed</u>
   - (B) clo<u>set</u>
   - (C) stor<u>ms</u>
   - (D) tele<u>vision</u>

4. Which of these words does not have a suffix?
   - (F) runner
   - (G) untie
   - (H) hairless
   - (J) washable

5. Which of these words does not have a prefix?
   - (A) defrost
   - (B) nonstop
   - (C) fixable
   - (D) prepay

6. What does the prefix *un-* mean in the word *unsafe*?
   - (F) over
   - (G) not
   - (H) in favor of
   - (J) before

7. What does the suffix *-less* mean in the word *hopeless*?
   - (A) full of
   - (B) like
   - (C) place
   - (D) without

STOP

Reading

1.0

For pages 8–14

Mini-Test 1

DIRECTIONS: Choose the answer that means the same as the underlined word.

1. <u>Fearless</u> dog
   - (A) careless
   - (B) energetic
   - (C) unafraid
   - (D) sincere

2. <u>Solar</u> energy
   - (F) sun-powered
   - (G) sunburn
   - (H) electric
   - (J) powerful

DIRECTIONS: Find the sentence in which the underlined word is used in the same way.

3. **The <u>field</u> is planted with corn.**
   - (A) The field of technology is always changing.
   - (B) We can see deer in the field by our house.
   - (C) Her field is nursing.
   - (D) Our field trip is next Thursday.

4. **The <u>general</u> idea was to weave a basket.**
   - (F) She is a general in the army.
   - (G) The soldiers followed their general into battle.
   - (H) I think that the general had the best idea.
   - (J) No general study of history can cover everything.

DIRECTIONS: Choose the answer that means the opposite of the underlined word.

5. **He decided to <u>continue</u>.**
   - (A) stop
   - (B) go on
   - (C) roost
   - (D) sleep

6. **She was a <u>mighty</u> warrior.**
   - (F) great
   - (G) strong
   - (H) famous
   - (J) weak

DIRECTIONS: Read each sentence. Find the phrase where the underlined word is spelled incorrectly. Choose "No mistakes" if the phrase is correct.

7.
   - (A) The two <u>girls</u>
   - (B) <u>jumped</u> into the pool
   - (C) with a <u>huje</u> splash.
   - (D) No mistakes

8.
   - (F) My favorite <u>samwich</u>
   - (G) is peanut <u>butter</u>
   - (H) and <u>grape</u> jelly.
   - (J) No mistakes

9.
   - (A) Pam's <u>dollhouse</u>
   - (B) has real <u>lites</u>
   - (C) and a <u>staircase</u>.
   - (D) No mistakes

Reading Standards

2.0 Reading Comprehension

Students read and understand grade-level-appropriate material. They draw upon a variety of comprehension strategies as needed (e.g., generating and responding to essential questions, making predictions, comparing information from several sources).

Structural Features of Informational Materials

2.1 Use titles, tables of contents, chapter headings, glossaries, and indexes to locate information in text. *(See page 17.)*

What it means:

Structural Features of Informational Materials

● Students should be familiar with the parts of a book and how to use them to find information and answer questions.

Comprehension and Analysis of Grade-Level-Appropriate Text

2.2 Ask questions and support answers by connecting prior knowledge with literal information found in, and inferred from, the text. *(See page 18.)*

2.3 Demonstrate comprehension by identifying answers in the text. *(See page 19.)*

2.4 Recall major points in the text and make and modify predictions about forthcoming information. *(See page 20.)*

2.5 Distinguish the main idea and supporting details in expository text. *(See page 21.)*

2.6 Extract appropriate and significant information from the text, including problems and solutions. *(See page 22.)*

What it means:

Comprehension and Analysis of Grade-Level-Appropriate Text

● As students read, they should use several strategies to help them understand the material more thoroughly. For example, students should be able to ask questions and give answers by connecting what they already know with the new information found in the text.

● Students' understanding of a text's major points should help them to look ahead and predict what will unfold next.

● Students should be able to identify the main idea and any supporting details in what they read.

2.7 Follow simple multiple-step written instructions (e.g., how to assemble a product or play a board game). *(See page 23.)*

Name _____ Date _____

Finding Information

 Clue | A table of contents is at the front of a book and gives you the name and page number of chapters or topics. An index is at the back of a book and gives page numbers of where specific information is found.

DIRECTIONS: Use the sample index for numbers 1–3.

> **O**
> Oak, 291–292
> Obsidian, 175–176
> Oceans, 361–375
>   density of, 363–364
>   life in, 367–370
>   waves, 371–372
>   temperature of, 365
> resources, 373–375

1. You will find information about what topic on page 365?

- (A) ocean temperatures
- (B) density of the ocean
- (C) waves
- (D) the octopus

2. On what pages will you most likely find information about mining the oceans for minerals?

- (F) pages 175–176
- (G) pages 368–369
- (H) pages 373–375
- (J) pages 371–372

3. You can read about octopuses on pages 368–369. This information is part of what section under *Oceans*?

- (A) resources
- (B) life in
- (C) waves
- (D) temperature

DIRECTIONS: Use the sample table of contents for numbers 4–6.

> **Table of Contents**
> 1 Animals Around the World 11
> 2 Zoos of the World 42
> 3 Creatures of the Sea 59
> 4 Rodents 85
> 5 Reptiles and Amphibians 101
> 6 Insects and Spiders 112

4. In which chapter would you most likely read about starfish, sea horses, and sharks?

- (F) Chapter 5
- (G) Chapter 1
- (H) Chapter 4
- (J) Chapter 3

5. Which chapter is the shortest?

- (A) Chapter 5
- (B) Chapter 2
- (C) Chapter 3
- (D) Chapter 1

6. In which chapter would you find information about honeybees?

- (F) 6
- (G) 5
- (H) 4
- (J) 3

STOP

Reading

2.2

Making Inferences

DIRECTIONS: Read the passage and answer the questions.

Traveling Seeds

Everyone knows that flowering plants cannot fly, run, or walk. But, through their seeds, they can move from place to place. That is why you see new plants growing each year where there were none before.

Flowering plants grow in many different colors and sizes, but they all have seeds. The part of the plant that holds the seeds is called the fruit. Some seeds travel in their fruit. Others fall out and travel to a place where they can grow. But how do they get to this new place?

Some seeds stick to people's clothes or animals' fur and are carried from place to place. The seeds drop off and form new plants where they fall. Other seeds may be scattered by wind and rain.

However it happens, seeds certainly move.

1. **Which of the following is not a way that seeds can travel to a new place?**

   (A) on your shirt

   (B) in the wind

   (C) on a walking plant

   (D) on a dog

2. **Number the sentences from 1 to 4 to summarize one way that seeds could move from place to place.**

   _____ Seeds stick to your shirt.

   _____ Seeds form new plants where they fall.

   _____ Seeds fall off of your shirt.

   _____ You walk in a garden.

3. **From the passage, you can conclude that seeds _____ move around.**

   (F) do

   (G) do not

4. **From the details in the passage, write a sentence to explain why you see new plants growing in places where there were none the year before.**

   _____

   _____

   _____

   _____

2.3

Recalling Details

DIRECTIONS: Read the passage and answer the questions.

A Solar Eclipse

Have you ever seen an eclipse of the sun? It is called a *solar eclipse*. *Solar* means *sun*. A solar eclipse happens when the sun's light is blocked from Earth. Do you know why this happens?

The moon travels around Earth. Earth and the moon both travel around the sun. Sometimes, the moon passes exactly between the sun and Earth. The sun's light is blocked by the moon. Earth becomes dark. This darkness can last from two to seven minutes. Then, as the moon moves, the sunlight appears again. A solar eclipse is an amazing event.

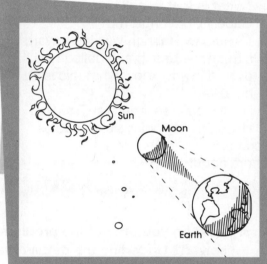

1. **Kwanda is writing a report on solar eclipses. Which sentence would help her summarize what a solar eclipse is?**

   Ⓐ Have you ever seen an eclipse of the sun?

   Ⓑ A solar eclipse happens when the sun's light is blocked from Earth.

   Ⓒ The moon travels around Earth.

   Ⓓ Then, as the moon moves, the sunlight appears again.

2. **The word *solar* means _____.**

   Ⓕ moon

   Ⓖ blocked

   Ⓗ eclipse

   Ⓙ sun

3. **Which of the following statements about a solar eclipse is not true?**

   Ⓐ The darkness of an eclipse lasts a day.

   Ⓑ The sunlight appears again when the moon moves.

   Ⓒ Sometimes the moon passes exactly between the sun and the Earth.

   Ⓓ Earth and the moon both travel around the sun.

STOP

Reading
Reading Comprehension

2.4

Identifying Major Points

DIRECTIONS: Read the story and answer the questions.

At the Water's Edge

Gabe walked down to the water. The sun was setting. The sky was blazing with orange, yellow, pink, and red. At the edge of the water was an odd-looking creature about one-foot long. Its body seemed to be in three parts. A long, hard, pointed tail poked its way out of its body. "What is that thing?" wondered Gabe. "Can it hurt me?"

He saw Hannah walking toward him on the beach and called her over. "Do you know what this is?" he asked.

"It's a horseshoe crab," replied Hannah. "My older sister studies them. She knows a lot about horseshoe crabs."

"Great," said Gabe. "I want to know more about them."

1. **What time of day does the story take place?**

   _____

2. **Where does the story take place?**

   _____

3. **List the characters in the story.**

   _____

   _____

4. **Name the problem(s) Gabe encounters in the story.**

   _____

   _____

   _____

5. **How do you predict the problem will be solved? Underline the details that helped you decide this.**

   _____

   _____

   _____

   _____

   _____

   _____

   _____

   _____

   _____

The Main Idea and Supporting Details

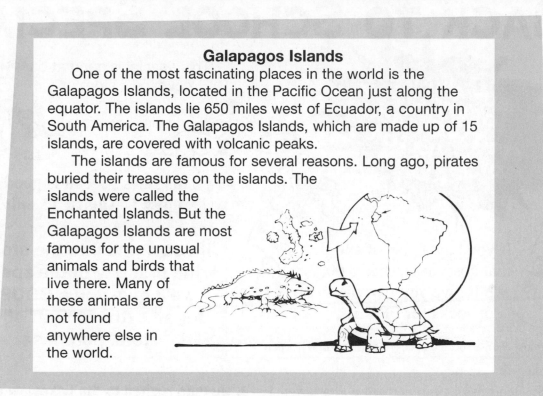

Galapagos Islands

One of the most fascinating places in the world is the Galapagos Islands, located in the Pacific Ocean just along the equator. The islands lie 650 miles west of Ecuador, a country in South America. The Galapagos Islands, which are made up of 15 islands, are covered with volcanic peaks.

The islands are famous for several reasons. Long ago, pirates buried their treasures on the islands. The islands were called the Enchanted Islands. But the Galapagos Islands are most famous for the unusual animals and birds that live there. Many of these animals are not found anywhere else in the world.

DIRECTIONS: Read the passage and fill in the web with information about the Galapagos Islands. For each major detail, add supporting details.

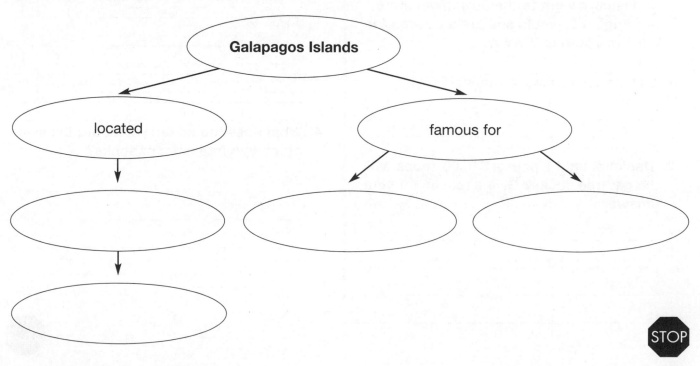

2.6

Problems and Solutions

BACK TO SCHOOL SPECIAL

BUY A PAIR OF SHOES. GET TWO PAIRS OF SOCKS FOR FREE!

If you buy a pair of shoes that costs at least $20.00, we'll give you two pairs of socks for FREE!*

*You must choose socks that cost less than $2.00 per pair

This special is good at our downtown store only, not at our Lakeview store.

This sales special is good from August 1–August 15 only.

If you come into the store on the first day of the special, we'll give you a COUPON for an extra 10% off of your total purchase.

DIRECTIONS: Read this advertisement and answer the questions.

1. If Jessalyn went to the downtown store on August 5, would she get a coupon for an extra 10% off? Why?

   _____

   _____

   _____

2. Daniel bought a pair of $15.00 shoes. Will he get free socks? Give a reason for your answer.

   _____

   _____

   _____

   _____

3. Juanita rushed to the Lakeview store on August 1. Will she get the sock special? Give a reason for your answer.

   _____

   _____

   _____

   _____

4. What does the ad tell you about the value of the two free pairs of socks?

   _____

   _____

   _____

   _____

STOP

2.7

Following Instructions

DIRECTIONS: Read the directions for making a piñata and answer the questions.

A Mexican Fiesta

A common sight at parties (or *fiestas*) in Mexico is the *piñata*, a hanging decoration filled with candies, fruits, and small gifts. You can make your own piñata by following the directions below.

1. Inflate a balloon.
2. Dip strips of newspaper into paste (made of flour and water), and cover the balloon. Let dry.
3. To make animal features or other shapes, use twisted rolls of newspaper and cover them with the paste strips. Be sure to leave a small opening to use later for filling the piñata with prizes.
4. Allow the piñata to dry.
5. Decorate the piñata with paint or small pieces of colored tissue paper that can be glued in different designs.
6. Pop the balloon inside the piñata. Fill the piñata with candies, fruits, and prizes. Use heavy-duty tape or newspaper strips to seal the filling hole.
7. Hang your piñata using string or wire.
8. Ask players to line up. Blindfold the first player and give him or her a small stick. Lead the player to the piñata and tell the player to begin hitting it when you say "Go!"

1. **What is the correct order for making a piñata?**

   (A) allow to dry, fill with prizes, hang it up

   (B) dip strips of newspaper into paste, fill with prizes, inflate balloon

   (C) cover the balloon, decorate, allow to dry

   (D) allow to dry, decorate, inflate balloon

2. **True or false? You should be sure not to pop the balloon inside the piñata after it dries.**

   _____

3. **Marguerita is ready to fill a piñata with prizes but there is no hole to pour them inside. Which step was skipped by the person who made the piñata?**

   _____

STOP

Reading

2.0

Mini-Test 2

For pages 17–23

DIRECTIONS: Read the passage and answer the questions.

Sign Language

Sign language is used by people who are not able to hear or speak well. They use their hands instead of their voices to talk. Their hand signals may be different letters, words, or whole ideas.

Sign language is used by other people, too. Have you ever watched a football or basketball game? The referees use hand signals to let people know what has happened in the game. Signs can mean "foul," "time out," or can let players know when a play was good.

Guess who else uses sign language? You do! You wave your hand for *hello* and *goodbye*. You nod your head up and down to say *yes* and back and forth to say *no*. You point to show which way to go. Sign language is used by people everywhere as another way of communicating.

1. **What is the main idea of this passage?**

   (A) Sign language is used by people who cannot hear well.

   (B) Sign language is important to many sports.

   (C) Sign language is not used in all countries.

   (D) Sign language is used by people everywhere.

2. **What is one example of sign language?**

   (F) calling out the name of your friend

   (G) singing a song

   (H) waving *hello* or *goodbye*

   (J) talking on the telephone

3. **What is another example of sign language?**

   (A) rocking a baby to sleep

   (B) raising your hand in class

   (C) running down the sidewalk to school

   (D) jumping rope

4. **Which sentence is an opinion?**

   (F) Sign language is used as another way of communicating.

   (G) Sign language is very interesting.

   (H) Sign language is used in sports.

   (J) Sign language is done with hand signals.

Reading Standards

3.0 Literary Response and Analysis

Students read and respond to a wide variety of significant works of children's literature. They distinguish between the structural features of the text and literary terms or elements (e.g., theme, plot, setting, characters).

Structural Features of Literature

3.1 Distinguish common forms of literature (e.g., poetry, drama, fiction, nonfiction). *(See page 26.)*

Narrative Analysis of Grade-Level-Appropriate Text

3.2 Comprehend basic plots of classic fairy tales, myths, folktales, legends, and fables from around the world. *(See page 27.)*

3.3 Determine what characters are like by what they say or do and by how the author or illustrator portrays them. *(See page 28.)*

3.4 Determine the underlying theme or author's message in fiction and nonfiction text. *(See page 29.)*

3.5 Recognize the similarities of sounds in words and rhythmic patterns (e.g., alliteration, onomatopoeia) in a selection. *(See page 30.)*

What it means:

Narrative Analysis of Grade-Level-Appropriate Text

- Students should be able to explain an author's purpose in a written work. For example, did the author want to tell a story, express an opinion, inform, entertain, or persuade?
- Students should recognize the use of alliteration, which is the repetition of the sound at the beginning of words (e.g., Seven seahorses swam in the sea.). Students should also recognize the use of onomatopoeia, which is the use of words that suggest the sound of what they describe (e.g., The bee *buzzed*.).

3.6 Identify the speaker or narrator in a selection. *(See page 31.)*

Reading
3.1

Identifying Types of Literature

DIRECTIONS: Read the passage and answer the questions.

Lunch Guests

It was a sunny spring day. Kaye and her friend Tasha were walking in the woods. As they walked, they noticed many squirrels ahead of them running in the same direction.

"Let's follow them and see where they are going," said Tasha.

"Great idea!" exclaimed Kaye, and the two girls raced ahead.

Soon they came to a large clearing in the forest. There were hundreds and hundreds of squirrels—more squirrels than either girl had ever seen. As they stared in amazement at the scene before them, a plump gray squirrel with a fluffy tail skittered over to them and said politely, "Would you care to join us for lunch?"

Tasha and Kaye were stunned into silence. But after a moment, they looked at each other, shrugged, and said, "Why not?" They both liked nuts.

1. This passage is which genre (type) of literature?

   (A) poetry

   (B) fiction

   (C) biography

   (D) fable

2. What clues in the story helped you decide what genre it is?

   _____

   _____

   _____

   _____

   _____

3. Using the passage as an example, write a definition of this genre. Use the sentences below as a guide.

   _____ is usually a story about

   _____

   _____

   _____

   _____ includes details about

   _____

   _____

   _____

Reading

3.2

Literary Response
and Analysis

Understanding Plots

DIRECTIONS: Read the passage and answer the questions.

The Goldilocks Report

At 5:05 P.M. we were called to the home of a Mr. and Mrs. Bear. They had been out for the day. Upon returning, they found the lock on their door had been broken. Officer Paws and I went into the house. We found that food had been stolen and a chair had been broken.

Paws searched the backyard while I went upstairs. I found a person asleep in a small bed. The subject was a female human with curly blonde hair. She was unknown to the Bear family. The human claimed her name was Goldilocks. She could not prove that fact. She was taken to the police station for questioning.

Officer Grizzly

1. **In the fairy tale "Goldilocks and the Three Bears," who is the main character?**

   (A) Goldilocks

   (B) Baby Bear

   (C) Papa Bear

   (D) Officer Grizzly

2. **How is the "The Goldilocks Report" different from the fairy tale?**

   (F) a chair was broken

   (G) it's a police report

   (H) food was stolen

   (J) it uses bears as characters

3. **Which character tells the story of "The Goldilocks Report"?**

   (A) Goldilocks

   (B) Baby Bear

   (C) Papa Bear

   (D) Officer Grizzly

4. **Which character is in the fairy tale but not in "The Goldilocks Report"?**

   (F) Paws

   (G) Papa Bear

   (H) Mama Bear

   (J) Baby Bear

STOP

Reading

3.3

Understanding Characters

DIRECTIONS: Read the two passages and answer the questions.

A Day on the Trail

Dylan's Story:

Today was the day I had been waiting for—our class nature hike. Before we left the bus, Mr. Evans told us the person who found the most items on the list would get a prize. A lot of the kids didn't understand that they needed to be quiet to see any wildlife. I stayed behind the group and moved very slowly down the trail. I found sixteen different leaf specimens and did scratch tests on five different rocks. I was sorry when we had to leave, but I was thrilled to win a field microscope!

Danny's Story:

Today was the day I had been dreading—our class nature hike. My mother could barely drag me out of bed. On the bus, Mr. Evans handed out lists we were supposed to fill in. As if the hike itself wasn't bad enough, I lost my canteen right away; then I ripped my t-shirt on a bush. I did manage to find a couple of rocks, but only because I tripped on them. I didn't see even one animal. By the time we got back to the bus, I was hot, dirty, and tired. To make things worse, I was covered with poison ivy.

1. **Write in the name of the character described by each phrase.**

   (A) _____ thrilled to win a microscope

   (B) _____ saw no animals

   (C) _____ got up late

   (D) _____ found five different rocks

2. **Whose day was exciting, interesting, happy, and good?**

   _____

   _____

3. **The two characters reacted very differently to the same setting. Which character's reaction was most like yours would be? Why?**

   _____

   _____

   _____

   _____

   _____

   _____

   _____

   _____

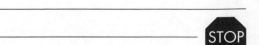

Reading
3.4

The Author's Message

DIRECTIONS: Read the passage and answer the questions.

Animal Mysteries

As long as people have studied animals, they have wondered about why animals act certain ways. Animal behavior can be a real mystery.

One mystery has to do with some animals' strange behavior before earthquakes. Horses and cattle stampede, seabirds screech, dogs howl, and some animals even come out of hibernation early before an earthquake begins.

Another mystery involves birds and ants. No one can explain why a bird will pick up an ant in its beak and rub the ant over its feathers again and again. This is called "anting," and birds have been known to do this for an hour without stopping.

One animal mystery is very sad. For hundreds of years, some whales have swum into shallow waters and mysteriously grounded themselves on a beach where they might die. Reports of beached whales occur about five times a year somewhere in the world.

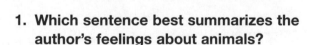

1. **Which sentence best summarizes the author's feelings about animals?**

   (A) She is curious about animals.

   (B) She understands animals completely.

   (C) She does not like animals.

   (D) She wishes animals were quieter.

2. **What word(s) in the passage helped you guess how the author felt about animals?**

   _____

   _____

3. **The author most likely has written this passage to _____.**

   (F) study animal behavior before earthquakes

   (G) explain why whales beach themselves

   (H) explain why birds rub ants on their feathers

   (J) tell readers about some interesting animal mysteries

Reading
3.5

Sounds and Rhythms

DIRECTIONS: Finish this poem by choosing the right words to fill the blanks.

> *A cow is such a silly thing,*
> *It makes a silly sound, _____ (1) _____*
> *It lives on a _____ (2) _____*
> *Inside a barn*
> *And gives us milk, _____ (3) _____ .*

1. Ⓐ bark
   Ⓑ meow
   Ⓒ oink
   Ⓓ moo

2. Ⓕ beach
   Ⓖ farm
   Ⓗ street
   Ⓙ porch

3. Ⓐ too
   Ⓑ also
   Ⓒ yum
   Ⓓ wow

DIRECTIONS: *Roar* is a word that sounds like the sound it names. Which of these words sounds like the sound it names?

4. Ⓕ catch
   Ⓖ beep
   Ⓗ drive
   Ⓙ loud

5. Ⓐ burn
   Ⓑ open
   Ⓒ fly
   Ⓓ chirp

6. Ⓕ run
   Ⓖ purple
   Ⓗ buzz
   Ⓙ empty

DIRECTIONS: Finish this poem by filling in the blank with the correct rhyming word.

> *When the telephone rang,*
> *I was sound asleep.*
> *I cleared my throat,*
> *and began to _____ .*

7. Ⓐ sing
   Ⓑ snore
   Ⓒ speak
   Ⓢ wake

STOP

Reading

3.6

Identifying the Speaker

Literary Response
and Analysis

DIRECTIONS: Read the paragraphs and answer the questions.

Samantha's Birthday

A. I knew it would be a great day from the minute I woke up. Piled beside my bed was a stack of presents. I jumped out of bed. I was so excited. When I came downstairs carrying the presents, my sister shouted, "Happy birthday!"

B. Before Samantha woke up, I left her presents beside her bed. I knew she would like the surprise from her father and me. When we saw Samantha on the stairs, we surprised her by saying, "Happy birthday!"

C. I bought Samantha a book about dinosaurs for her birthday. Mom and Dad let me do extra chores to earn the money. I had to wake up early to surprise her but it was worth it to see her face when we all said, "Happy birthday!"

1. Who is the writer of passage A?

_____

What special day is it for this person?

_____

2. Who is the writer of passage B?

_____

How did you guess?

_____

_____

_____

3. Who is the writer of passage C?

_____

How did you guess?

_____

_____

_____

_____

_____

_____

_____

Reading

3.0

For pages 26–31

Mini-Test 3

DIRECTIONS: Choose the best answer.

1. **Which of these sentences would most likely be found in a mystery story?**

    (A) The President lives in Washington.

    (B) Bears eat many different foods.

    (C) Dolores opened the door slowly, but no one was there.

    (D) Before you can fix a leaky roof, you must find the leak.

2. **Yesterday morning, the governor signed the bill that will set aside five million dollars for state parks.**

    This sentence would most likely be found in a _____.

    (F) biography

    (G) newspaper article

    (H) fairy tale

    (J) mystery

3. **Robbie got up early without anyone waking him. Today, he and the rest of the family were going fishing at Parker Lake. Robbie loved fishing, and Parker Lake had the best fishing around. They were going to spend the whole day on the lake. He was sure he would catch a big one.**

    How do you think Robbie feels?

    (A) worried

    (B) proud

    (C) excited

    (D) disappointed

4. **By the time the mayor came to judge the snow sculptures, Carlos had finished his. He had made a robot and had used tennis balls for eyes. "This is the most original sculpture I've seen," said the mayor. "Those are great eyes." He handed Carlos a blue ribbon.**

    How do you think Carlos feels at the end of the story?

    (F) scared

    (G) proud

    (H) sad

    (J) angry

5. **I took Daniel to the dentist. The dentist cleaned his teeth and told me there were no cavities. I was proud of my son for taking such good care of his teeth!**

    Who wrote this?

    (A) Daniel

    (B) Daniel's mother

    (C) the dentist

    (D) Daniel's brother

6. **Our ball bounced over the wall and into the neighbor's yard.**

    What are the two rhyming words in this sentence?

    (F) ball and yard

    (G) wall and yard

    (H) ball and wall

    (J) ball and bounced

STOP

32

How Am I Doing?

Mini-Test 1	8–9 answers correct	**Great Job!** Move on to the section test on page 34.
Page 15 **Number Correct**	5–7 answers correct	**You're almost there!** But you still need a little practice. Review practice pages 8–14 before moving on to the section test on page 34.
	0–4 answers correct	**Oops!** Time to review what you have learned and try again. Review the practice section on pages 8–14. Then retake the test on page 15. Now move on to the section test on page 34.
Mini-Test 2	4 answers correct	**Awesome!** Move on to the section test on page 34.
Page 24 **Number Correct**	3 answers correct	**You're almost there!** But you still need a little practice. Review practice pages 17–23 before moving on to the section test on page 34.
	0–2 answers correct	**Oops!** Time to review what you have learned and try again. Review the practice section on pages 17–23. Then retake the test on page 24. Now move on to the section test on page 34.
Mini-Test 3	6 answers correct	**Great Job!** Move on to the section test on page 34.
Page 32 **Number Correct**	4–5 answers correct	**You're almost there!** But you still need a little practice. Review practice pages 26–31 before moving on to the section test on page 34.
	0–3 answers correct	**Oops!** Time to review what you have learned and try again. Review the practice section on pages 26–31. Then retake the test on page 32. Now move on to the section test on page 34.

Name _____   Date _____

Final Reading Test
for pages 8–32

1. **Find the answer that means the same or about the same as the underlined word.**

   long <u>journey</u>

   Ⓐ story

   Ⓑ movie

   Ⓒ road

   Ⓓ trip

2. **Find the word that means the opposite of the underlined word.**

   <u>thrilling</u> ride

   Ⓕ long

   Ⓖ exciting

   Ⓗ boring

   Ⓙ interesting

3. **Read the sentence with the missing word and then read the question. Find the best answer to the question.**

   The weather will _____ tomorrow.

   Which word means the weather will get better?

   Ⓐ improve

   Ⓑ change

   Ⓒ worsen

   Ⓓ vary

4. **Choose the word that correctly completes both sentences.**

   Who will _____ this problem?

   The _____ on the shovel is broken.

   Ⓕ solve

   Ⓖ blade

   Ⓗ cause

   Ⓙ handle

5. **Find the word that fits best in the blank.**

   Dogs need _____ to stay healthy.

   Ⓐ treats

   Ⓑ dishes

   Ⓒ exercise

   Ⓓ leashes

6. **Find the underlined word that is <u>not</u> spelled correctly.**

   Ⓕ easy <u>lesson</u>

   Ⓖ <u>quiet</u> room

   Ⓗ last <u>forevr</u>

   Ⓙ <u>private</u> property

7. **Find the word that has the same vowel sound as the underlined part of this word.**

   cr<u>i</u>sp

   Ⓐ pinch

   Ⓑ stair

   Ⓒ lion

   Ⓓ cried

8. **Which word in this sentence has a prefix?**

   The largest bottle of ketchup was unopened.

   Ⓕ largest

   Ⓖ bottle

   Ⓗ ketchup

   Ⓙ unopened

GO

9. **Which word in this sentence has a suffix?**
   Alisha was ill and quietly left the party.

   (A) ill

   (B) quietly

   (C) left

   (D) party

10. **Which word could be a heading for the other three words?**

   (F) fly

   (G) insect

   (H) ant

   (J) beetle

11. **Which word is first in the dictionary?**

   (A) reef

   (B) relief

   (C) real

   (D) repeat

12. **Which word is last in the dictionary?**

   (F) plural

   (G) park

   (H) princess

   (J) pumpkin

13. **Read the dictionary entry. Which definition best fits the word** <u>express</u> **as it is used in the sentence below?**

   The <u>express</u> **will get us home quickly.**

   ex·press [ik spres´] *v.* **1.** to put into words **2.** to show or reveal **3.** to send quickly *adj.* **4.** clear or easily understood **5.** quick *n.* **6.** a direct train

   (A) 1

   (B) 2

   (C) 5

   (D) 6

14. **Sally is reading a book called** *Home Gardening for Young People.* **Which of these sentences would most likely be at the beginning of the book?**

   (F) After you have planted the seeds, you'll have to keep them watered so they don't dry out.

   (G) Few things are as rewarding as tending a garden.

   (H) Now comes the fun part, eating vegetables you have raised.

   (J) The most difficult part of having a garden is making sure that weeds don't take over.

15. **Which sentence is most likely to come next in the story below?**

   The travelers found themselves in a forest of talking trees. Just then, all the trees began talking at once. They were so loud that it was impossible to understand what they were saying.

   (A) Once upon a time, a group of travelers started on a long journey.

   (B) No one knew where they were, and they became frightened.

   (C) Suddenly, the biggest tree said, "Quiet, everyone!"

   (D) The outside of the trunk of a tree is called the bark.

GO

16. Where would this sentence most likely be found?

What I remember most about that big old house in Iowa was the kitchen, a room that was always warm and always smelled wonderful.

- (F) a newspaper article
- (G) an autobiography
- (H) a fairy tale
- (J) a science book

For numbers 17–24, read the passage. Choose the best answer for each question.

Wendy Lost and Found

Wendy was scared. For the second time in her young life, she was lost. When the branch fell on her small house and the fence, she had barely escaped. She leaped across the fallen fence into the woods. Now the rain poured down and the wind howled. The little woodchuck shivered under a big oak tree. She did not know what to do.

When Wendy was a baby, her mother had died. She had been alone in the woods then, too. She could not find enough food. Then she hurt her paw. All day she scratched at a small hole in the ground, trying to make a burrow. Every night, she was hungry.

One day, Rita had found her. Rita had knelt down by Wendy's shallow burrow and set down an apple. Wendy limped slowly out and took the apple. It was the best thing she had ever tasted. Rita took the baby woodchuck to the wildlife center, and Wendy had lived there ever since. Most of the animals at the center were orphans. Rita taught them how to live in the wild, and then let them go when they were ready. But Wendy's paw did not heal well, and Rita knew that Wendy would never be able to go back to the wild. So Rita had made Wendy a house and a pen. Wendy even had a job—she visited schools with Rita so that students could learn all about woodchucks.

Now the storm had ruined Wendy's house. She did not know how to find Rita. At dawn, the rain ended. Wendy limped down to a big stream and sniffed the air. Maybe the center was across the stream. Wendy jumped onto a rock and then hopped to another one. She landed on her bad paw and fell into the fast-moving water. The little woodchuck struggled to keep her nose above water. The current tossed her against a tangle of branches. Wendy held on with all her might.

"There she is!" Wendy heard Rita's voice. Rita and Ben, another worker from the wildlife center, were across the stream. Rita waded out to the branches, lifted Wendy up, and wrapped her in a blanket. Wendy purred her thanks. By the time Ben and Rita got into the van to go back to the center, Wendy was fast asleep.

17. This story is mostly about _____.

- (A) a wildlife center worker
- (B) a woodchuck who lives at a wildlife center
- (C) a woodchuck who can do tricks
- (D) a woodchuck who learns how to swim

18. How does the story start?

- (F) with Wendy's life as a baby
- (G) in the middle of the storm
- (H) with Wendy's visit to school
- (J) when Wendy is in the stream

19. Why do you think the author wrote about Wendy's life as a baby?

- (A) so the reader knows that Wendy has been lost before and knows what to do
- (B) so the reader knows that Wendy can't live in the wild and is in danger
- (C) so the reader knows that Wendy trusts people and will be all right
- (D) so the reader knows that Wendy can find apples to eat

GO

20. Which answer is a fact about woodchucks from the story?

- (F) Wendy loves apples.
- (G) Woodchucks dig burrows.
- (H) Woodchucks can climb tall fences.
- (J) Wendy limps because of her hurt paw.

21. What is the problem in the story "Wendy Lost and Found"?

- (A) Wendy hurt her paw.
- (B) Wendy got lost as a baby.
- (C) Wendy gets lost during a big storm.
- (D) Wendy does not trust Ben.

22. What are the settings for this story?

- (F) the woods and the wildlife center
- (G) the school and the stream
- (H) the school and the woods
- (J) the wildlife center and Rita's house

23. What is Rita's job?

- (A) saving woodchucks from streams
- (B) teaching science at a school
- (C) gathering apples
- (D) working at the wildlife center with animals

24. What is the climax of the story?

- (F) when Wendy's mother dies
- (G) when Rita gives Wendy an apple
- (H) when Wendy falls into the stream
- (J) when Rita wraps Wendy in a blanket

DIRECTIONS: Choose the best answer.

25. Jellyfish come in all sizes and colors. Some are only one inch across. Other jellyfish are five feet wide. Some are orange. Others are red. Some jellyfish have no color at all. Gently poke one type of jellyfish with a stick and it will glow. But don't let any jellyfish touch you, because they can sting!

The main idea of this passage is _____.

- (A) jellyfish can sting
- (B) some jellyfish are orange
- (C) there are many kinds of jellyfish
- (D) jellyfish can hide

26. Lynn was invited to a costume party. There was going to be a prize for the funniest costume. Lynn went as a clown. When she got to the party, she looked at what the others were wearing. Lynn said, "I guess a lot of people think a clown's costume is funny!"

From this story, what can you guess about the costumes at the party?

- (F) A lot of people had red and white costumes.
- (G) Lynn was the only person dressed as a clown.
- (H) Lynn was not the only person dressed as a clown.
- (J) Most people had worn costumes.

STOP

Name _____   Date _____

Reading Test
Answer Sheet

1. (A) (B) (C) (D)
2. (F) (G) (H) (J)
3. (A) (B) (C) (D)
4. (F) (G) (H) (J)
5. (A) (B) (C) (D)
6. (F) (G) (H) (J)
7. (A) (B) (C) (D)
8. (F) (G) (H) (J)
9. (A) (B) (C) (D)
10. (F) (G) (H) (J)

11. (A) (B) (C) (D)
12. (F) (G) (H) (J)
13. (A) (B) (C) (D)
14. (F) (G) (H) (J)
15. (A) (B) (C) (D)
16. (F) (G) (H) (J)
17. (A) (B) (C) (D)
18. (F) (G) (H) (J)
19. (A) (B) (C) (D)
20. (F) (G) (H) (J)

21. (A) (B) (C) (D)
22. (F) (G) (H) (J)
23. (A) (B) (C) (D)
24. (F) (G) (H) (J)
25. (A) (B) (C) (D)
26. (F) (G) (H) (J)

Writing Standards

1.0 Writing Strategies

Students write clear and coherent sentences and paragraphs that develop a central idea. Their writing shows they consider the audience and purpose. Students progress through the stages of the writing process (e.g., prewriting, drafting, revising, editing successive versions)

Organization and Focus

1.1 Create a single paragraph: *(See page 40.)*
   a. Develop a topic sentence.
   b. Include simple supporting facts and details.

Penmanship

1.2 Write legibly in cursive or joined italic, allowing margins and correct spacing between letters in a word and words in a sentence.

Research

1.3 Understand the structure and organization of various reference materials (e.g., dictionary, thesaurus, atlas, encyclopedia). *(See page 41.)*

Evaluation and Revision

1.4 Revise drafts to improve the coherence and logical progression of ideas by using an established rubric. *(See page 42.)*

What it means:

Evaluation and Revision

- A rubric is a set of guidelines that tells students what is expected on a particular task. It is often used as a basis for grading an assignment. By reviewing these guidelines, students can identify areas of their work that need improvement.
- The draft should fit the purpose (e.g., to inform, entertain, tell a story, etc.) and the audience (e.g., Writing directed to a group of peers would be different than writing directed to an adult.).
- Sentences should be clear and flow in a logical order.

Writing

1.1 # The Writing Process: Organizing

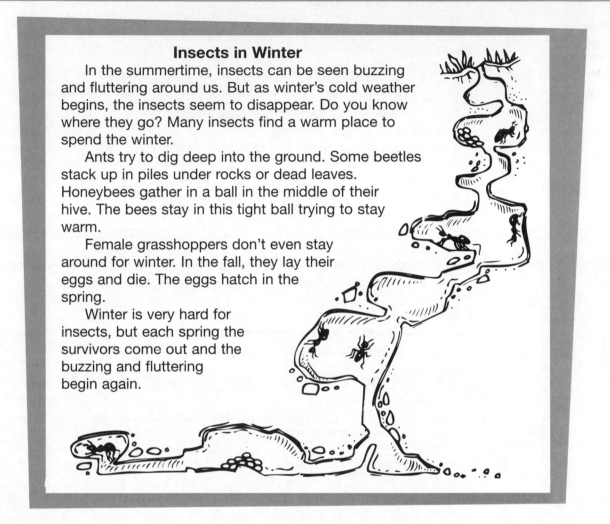

Insects in Winter

In the summertime, insects can be seen buzzing and fluttering around us. But as winter's cold weather begins, the insects seem to disappear. Do you know where they go? Many insects find a warm place to spend the winter.

Ants try to dig deep into the ground. Some beetles stack up in piles under rocks or dead leaves. Honeybees gather in a ball in the middle of their hive. The bees stay in this tight ball trying to stay warm.

Female grasshoppers don't even stay around for winter. In the fall, they lay their eggs and die. The eggs hatch in the spring.

Winter is very hard for insects, but each spring the survivors come out and the buzzing and fluttering begin again.

DIRECTIONS: Use the passage to fill in the topic sentence below. Fill in the rest of the ovals with supporting details.

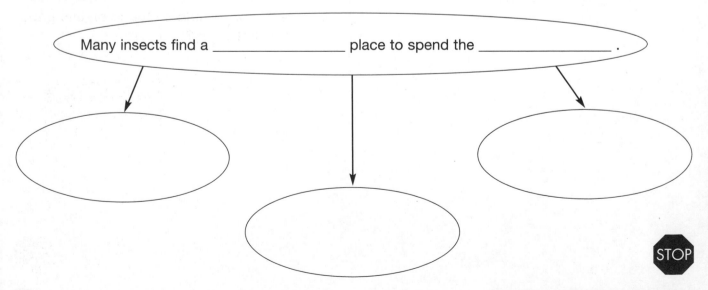

Many insects find a _____ place to spend the _____ .

Writing

1.3

The Writing Process: Research

Examples:

A Which of these words comes first in the dictionary?

- (A) damp
- (B) darn
- (C) dale
- (D) den

Answer: (C)

B Look at the guide words. Which word would be found on this page of the dictionary?

guide words
apple–assume

- (F) arctic
- (G) ape
- (H) aster
- (J) assure

Answer: (F)

DIRECTIONS: Which of these words comes first in the dictionary?

1.
- (A) tiger
- (B) tin
- (C) tiny
- (D) tine

2.
- (F) this
- (G) thirty
- (H) thirsty
- (J) thirteen

3.
- (A) city
- (B) cider
- (C) cinder
- (D) cliff

4.
- (F) interesting
- (G) indeed
- (H) insurance
- (J) idea

5.
- (A) trip
- (B) trap
- (C) tip
- (D) truck

6. **Which word would be found on this page of the dictionary?**

guide words
branch–brown

- (F) brute
- (G) broken
- (H) burn
- (J) brake

7. **Which word would be found on this page of the dictionary?**

guide words
prize–pump

- (A) puppy
- (B) pet
- (C) protect
- (D) punish

8. **Which word would be found on this page of the dictionary?**

guide words
strawberry–stroll

- (F) stress
- (G) strong
- (H) stick
- (J) strum

STOP

Writing

1.4

The Writing Process: Revising

DIRECTIONS: Read the journal entry. Then answer numbers 1–6. If the sentence needs no changes, choose "Correct as it is."

(1) My parents and I, we are flying to Chicago tomorrow. (2) My father is attending a business conference. (3) While Dad is working, Mom and I am seeing the sights (4) Go to the top of the Hancock Building and the Water Tower. (5) We will visiting my Aunt Ruth, too. (6) I can hardly wait to go! (7) We were leaving at seven o'clock tomorrow morning.

1. Sentence 1 is best written—

(A) My parents and I are flying to Chicago tomorrow.

(B) My parents and I were flying to Chicago tomorrow.

(C) My parents and I, we flew to Chicago tomorrow.

(D) Correct as it is

2. Sentence 2 is best written—

(F) My father is attended a business conference.

(G) My father will attending a business conference.

(H) My father attends a business conference.

(J) Correct as it is

3. Sentence 3 is best written—

(A) While Dad working, Mom will see the sights.

(B) While Dad is working, Mom and I will see the sights.

(C) While Dad is working, Mom and I are seen the sights.

(D) Correct as it is

4. Sentence 5 is best written—

(F) We have visited my Aunt Ruth, too.

(G) We will be visiting my Aunt Ruth, too.

(H) We are visit my Aunt Ruth,

(J) Correct as it is

5. Sentence 7 is best written—

(A) We will leaving at seven o'clock tomorrow morning.

(B) We are leaving at seven o'clock tomorrow morning.

(C) We be leaving at seven o'clock tomorrow morning.

(D) Correct as it is.

6. Which of these is not a sentence?

(F) Sentence 1

(G) Sentence 3

(H) Sentence 4

(J) Sentence 7

STOP

Writing

1.0

For pages 40–42

Mini-Test 1

DIRECTIONS: Choose the best answer.

1. **Where would you look to find a map of Oregon?**
   - (A) in a newspaper
   - (B) in an atlas
   - (C) in a telephone book
   - (D) in a math book

2. **Where would you look to find out how *yesterday* is broken into syllables?**
   - (F) in a newspaper
   - (G) in a history book
   - (H) in a dictionary
   - (J) in an encyclopedia

3. **Where would you look to find information about sharks?**
   - (A) in a newspaper
   - (B) in a history book
   - (C) in a dictionary
   - (D) in an encyclopedia

DIRECTIONS: Choose the answer that develops the topic sentence in the best way.

4. **The canary is one of the best-liked of all pet birds.**
   - (F) Canaries are not only pretty, but they sing cheerful songs.
   - (G) Canaries can be yellow, red, or orange.
   - (H) You have to be careful with a pet bird, or it may escape.
   - (J) Canaries like to live in the Canary Islands.

DIRECTIONS: Read each paragraph. Choose the answer that would make the best topic sentence for the paragraph.

5. **_____. Both my mom and dad work, so they get in the bathroom first. My sister and I get up next. While we get ready, Dad fixes us breakfast.**
   - (A) Morning in our house is very busy.
   - (B) Breakfast is my favorite meal.
   - (C) My sister and I like to sleep in.
   - (D) We take a bus to school in the morning.

6. **_____. After President John Adams moved in, the outside was painted white. However, the name *White House* did not come into use until much later, when President Theodore Roosevelt had the name put on his writing paper.**
   - (F) The President's house was not always known as the White House.
   - (G) George Washington did not want to live in the White House.
   - (H) The White House was burned down during the War of 1812.
   - (J) President Roosevelt, who lived in the White House, loved to ride horses.

STOP

Writing Standards

2.0 Writing Applications (Genres and Their Characteristics)

Students write compositions that describe and explain familiar objects, events, and experiences. Student writing demonstrates a command of standard American English and the drafting, research, and organizational strategies outlined in Writing Standard 1.0.

Using the writing strategies of grade three outlined in Writing Standard 1.0, students:

2.1 Write narratives: *(See page 45.)*

    a. Provide a context within which an action takes place.

    b. Include well-chosen details to develop the plot.

    c. Provide insight into why the selected incident is memorable.

What it means:

- Students should be able to write a story about a familiar event. Narratives typically answer the question "What happened?"

2.2 Write descriptions that use concrete sensory details to present and support unified impressions of people, places, things, or experiences. *(See page 46.)*

What it means:

- Students should use details based on sight, smell, hearing, taste, or touch to draw the reader into the narrative and create coherent descriptions of characters and events.

2.3 Write personal and formal letters, thank-you notes, and invitations: *(See page 47.)*

    a. Show awareness of the knowledge and interests of the audience and establish a purpose and context.

    b. Include the date, proper salutation, body, closing, and signature.

Writing

2.1

Writing Narratives

DIRECTIONS: Read the short story about a friend's visit. Then think about a fiction story that you would like to write. Write one or two sentences to answer each question below.

> Juan looked at the clock. He paced across the floor. His best friend, Bill, was coming to visit for the first time in six months. Bill had moved very far away. Juan wondered if they would still feel like good friends.
>
> The doorbell rang, and Juan raced to answer it. Bill looked a bit unsure. Juan smiled and started talking just as he always had when they had lived near one another. He made Bill feel comfortable. As the day went on, it felt like old times.

1. Think about the main character. Who is it? What is he or she like?

_____

_____

_____

_____

_____

_____

_____

2. Where does the story take place? When does the story take place? Now? In the past? In the future?

_____

_____

_____

_____

_____

_____

3. What problem will the main character have? How will he or she try to solve the problem?

_____

_____

_____

_____

_____

_____

_____

_____

_____

_____

_____

_____

_____

STOP

Writing

2.2

Writing Descriptions

DIRECTIONS: Read the paragraph about one student's favorite class. Then write sentences to answer each question about your favorite class.

> My favorite class is art. I like to draw, and I like to paint. The teacher is very nice. He shows us how to do new things. I always look forward to this class. It would be even better if it were longer.

1. What is your favorite class?

_____

_____

_____

2. Why is it your favorite?

_____

_____

_____

_____

_____

_____

_____

_____

_____

_____

_____

3. What might make this class even better?

_____

_____

_____

_____

_____

_____

_____

_____

_____

_____

_____

_____

_____

_____

STOP

Writing

2.3

Written Correspondence

DIRECTIONS: Read the letter below. In the letter, a girl explains to her father why she should be allowed to try in-line skating. Think of something you would like to be allowed to do. Write a letter to someone explaining why you should be allowed to do it.

Dear Dad,
    I would like to try in-line skating. I know that you think it is not safe, but I would be very careful. I would follow every safety rule. I would wear a helmet, elbow pads, and knee pads. I would only skate in safe places. Please give me a chance.

Love,
Bonita

_____

_____

_____

_____

_____

_____

_____

_____

_____

_____

_____

_____

_____

_____

_____

_____

_____

_____

STOP

Writing

2.0

For pages 45–47

Mini-Test 2

1. Write a sentence using each of the words below. Use descriptive words to tell how something looks, feels, smells, or tastes.

   bird

   _____

   _____

   _____

   blanket

   _____

   _____

   _____

   fire

   _____

   _____

   _____

   ice cream

   _____

   _____

   _____

   _____

2. Write a short letter to someone that you know. Thank them for a gift or for something special that the person did for you.

   _____

   _____

   _____

   _____

   _____

   _____

   _____

   _____

   _____

   _____

   _____

   _____

   _____

   _____

   _____

   _____

   _____

   _____

   _____

   _____

   _____

How Am I Doing?

Mini-Test 1	6 answers correct	**Great Job!** Move on to the section test on page 50.
Page 43 **Number Correct**	4–5 answers correct	**You're almost there!** But you still need a little practice. Review practice pages 40–42 before moving on to the section test on page 50.
	0–3 answers correct	**Oops!** Time to review what you have learned and try again. Review the practice section on pages 40–42. Then retake the test on page 43. Now move on to the section test on page 50.
Mini-Test 2	2 answers correct	**Awesome!** Move on to the section test on page 50.
Page 48 **Number Correct**	1 answer correct	**You're almost there!** But you still need a little practice. Review practice pages 45–47 before moving on to the section test on page 50.
	0 answers correct	**Oops!** Time to review what you have learned and try again. Review the practice section on pages 45–47. Then retake the test on page 48. Now move on to the section test on page 50.

Final Writing Test
for pages 40–48

1. **Look at these guide words from a dictionary page.**

guide words
nice–note

Which word would be found on this page?

- (A) noise
- (B) nap
- (C) now
- (D) neither

2. **Which word would be found on this page?**

guide words
count–crisp

- (F) collect
- (G) celebrate
- (H) crane
- (J) crow

3. **Find the best topic sentence for this story.**

_____. Some sand looks white and seems to sparkle. Some sand may be light tan, black, or even pink. Sand has the same color as the rocks from which it was made. Looking at sand under a magnifying glass makes it possible to see the sparkling colors more clearly.

- (A) Sand can be made up of large or small grains.
- (B) All sand looks about the same.
- (C) Not all sand looks the same.
- (D) The color of sand is very important.

4. **Find the best topic sentence for this story.**

_____. They help keep bits of dust from getting into our eyes. They act as umbrellas, keeping the rain from our eyes. They also help shade our eyes from the sun. Like the frame around a beautiful painting, eyelashes play an important part in keeping our eyes safe.

- (F) Eyelashes can be blonde, brown, or black.
- (G) Eyelashes protect our eyes from harm.
- (H) Do you have long eyelashes?
- (J) Eyelashes can be straight or curled.

5. **Choose the answer that best supports this topic sentence.**

Some animals and insects are speedy creatures.

- (A) A hummingbird can fly 60 miles an hour, and a duck can fly twice that fast.
- (B) Snails move very slowly.
- (C) Ducks and hummingbirds are both birds.
- (D) Some animals are fast and some are slow.

GO

DIRECTIONS: For numbers 6–9, read the passage and answer the questions.

(1) Put about four spoonfuls of water and one spoonful of sugar in a very small, open bottle. (2) Paint the bottle red. (3) Then hang the bottle under an overhanging roof or near a window. (4) If you plant red flowers, they will help, too. (5) The tiny hummingbirds will come to drink the sugar water. (6) The hummingbird will think that the bright feeder is another flower, and the sugar water is flower nectar. (7) Hummingbirds like brightly colored flowers that have lots of nectar.

6. Choose the best topic sentence for this paragraph.

- (A) Here's how to attract hummingbirds to your backyard.
- (B) Hummingbirds are among the fastest flyers in the bird world.
- (C) Do you like hummingbirds?
- (D) Hummingbirds are colorful birds.

7. Choose a sentence to take out of the essay.

- (F) Sentence 1
- (G) Sentence 3
- (H) Sentence 4
- (J) Sentence 6

8. Choose a better place for Sentence 7.

- (A) Between Sentence 1 and Sentence 2
- (B) Between Sentence 2 and Sentence 3
- (C) Between Sentence 3 and Sentence 4
- (D) Between Sentence 5 and Sentence 6

9. Choose the best sentence to add to the end of the essay.

- (F) Hummingbirds are as brightly colored as the flowers they like best.
- (G) Hummingbirds are fast flyers and dart from place to place.
- (H) By building a simple feeder, you can help hummingbirds and enjoy them in your yard.
- (J) By building a simple feeder, you can trick hummingbirds.

DIRECTIONS: For numbers 10–12, read the paragraph and answer the questions.

(1) These people face some difficulties in looking at the world around them. (2) To the color-blind, for example, red and green look like the same colors. (3) A color-blind person might have trouble telling a ripe tomato from an unripe one. (4) There are also some people in the world who cannot see any colors. (5) To them, everything looks black, white, or gray.

10. Choose the best topic sentence for this paragraph.

- (A) People who cannot tell one color from another are said to be color-blind.
- (B) To these people, yellow and brown are the main colors they can see.
- (C) A color-blind person cannot see any colors.
- (D) Red and green are hard to tell apart.

GO

11. Choose the best last sentence for this paragraph.

(A) Color-blindness can make some tasks difficult.

(B) Color-blindness creates special challenges, but does not keep people from leading normal lives.

(C) People with color blindness look like other people.

(D) Some animals are color-blind, too.

12. Choose the best sentence to add between Sentences 3 and 4.

(F) These people might also have difficulty telling "stop" from "go" on a traffic light.

(G) Color-blindness can be measured with special tests.

(H) Color-blind people do not look different from other people.

(J) Color-blindness may be cured in the future with special glasses.

DIRECTIONS: Choose the best answer.

13. When you are writing a letter, which comes first?

(A) Dear Mr. Benson,

(B) Sincerely,

(C) January 23, 2003

(D) your signature

14. When you are writing a letter, which comes last?

(F) your signature

(G) January 23, 2003

(H) Dear Mr. Benson,

(J) Sincerely,

DIRECTIONS: Read this letter and answer the questions that follow.

Dear Mrs. Howard,

(1) The old library is small and has too few books. (2) We would like to raise enough money to add space and buy more books and some computers. (3) One way we are raising money is by asking business owners to let us sell T-shirts outside their stores. (4) We would set up a table near your door and sell our shirts on Saturday. (5) It won't cost you anything and we promise not to bother your customers. (6) Our school was named after the woman who was our town's first mayor.

15. Which sentence would best begin this letter?

(A) Many students want to read books but can't find them.

(B) Our school is raising money for a new library.

(C) Our school is one of the oldest in the state.

(D) Last week I visited your store.

16. Which of these could be added after sentence 4?

(F) You can play games on computers.

(G) Friday is a school day.

(H) My teacher is new to our school this year.

(J) The table would be set up from nine to four.

17. Which sentence does not belong in this letter?

(A) 1

(B) 3

(C) 5

(D) 6

18. Which of these could be added at the end of the letter?

(F) We also promise to clean everything up when we are finished.

(G) She was also the owner of the first store in town.

(H) Your store is very busy, and we know a lot of people will come to shop on Saturday.

(J) It doesn't take long to get from our school to your store, so I am sure we will be on time.

DIRECTIONS: Choose the sentences that best develop the topic sentence.

19. Traffic was terrible yesterday afternoon.

(A) Cars were backed up from the bridge all the way to the interstate. It took my parents almost an hour to get home from work.

(B) A truck crashed into the bridge over the river. The driver was not injured, but it will take several months to fix the bridge.

(C) Normally, it takes my parents about 20 minutes to get home. They work near each other and come home from work together.

(D) The bridge was damaged when a truck crashed into it. The truck was carrying wood and bricks for a new house.

DIRECTIONS: Choose the sentence that best fits in the blank.

20. We began feeding birds this winter. _____. The birds enjoy different kinds of seeds, peanuts, and even apples.

(F) It has snowed more than usual this year.

(G) Our state bird is the cardinal.

(H) You can buy bird food at many different stores.

(J) There isn't much food for them, especially if it snows.

21. My friend Dora lives in the apartment below us. _____. Dora's parents opened a restaurant just a few blocks from our building.

(A) Another friend, Seth, lives near school.

(B) Sometimes it is hard to make friends.

(C) Her family moved here a few months ago.

(D) My favorite food is pizza with everything on it.

22. The wind was howling and our clothes were soaked with rain. _____. We hoped that help would come soon.

(F) It was raining and windy.

(G) We huddled around the fire to keep warm.

(H) We were so happy to be home.

(J) Our rescuers gave us blankets and food.

STOP

Writing Test
Answer Sheet

1 (A) (B) (C) (D)
2 (F) (G) (H) (J)
3 (A) (B) (C) (D)
4 (F) (G) (H) (J)
5 (A) (B) (C) (D)
6 (F) (G) (H) (J)
7 (A) (B) (C) (D)
8 (F) (G) (H) (J)
9 (A) (B) (C) (D)
10 (F) (G) (H) (J)

11 (A) (B) (C) (D)
12 (F) (G) (H) (J)
13 (A) (B) (C) (D)
14 (F) (G) (H) (J)
15 (A) (B) (C) (D)
16 (F) (G) (H) (J)
17 (A) (B) (C) (D)
18 (F) (G) (H) (J)
19 (A) (B) (C) (D)
20 (F) (G) (H) (J)

21 (A) (B) (C) (D)
22 (F) (G) (H) (J)

Written and Oral English Language Conventions Standards

The standards for written and oral English language conventions have been placed between those for writing and for listening and speaking because these conventions are essential to both sets of skills.

1.0 Written and Oral English Language Conventions

Students write and speak with a command of standard English conventions appropriate to this grade level.

Sentence Structure

1.1 Understand and be able to use complete and correct declarative, interrogative, imperative, and exclamatory sentences in writing and speaking. *(See page 57.)*

What it means:

Sentence Structure

- Students should be able to use correct sentences in writing and speaking that make a statement, ask a question, give a command, or express strong emotion.

Grammar

1.2 Identify subjects and verbs that are in agreement and identify and use pronouns, adjectives, compound words, and articles correctly in writing and speaking. *(See page 58.)*

1.3 Identify and use past, present, and future verb tenses properly in writing and speaking. *(See page 59.)*

1.4 Identify and use subjects and verbs correctly in speaking and writing simple sentences. *(See page 60.)*

What it means:

Grammar

- Students should use singular verbs with singular subjects and plural verbs with plural subjects in writing and speaking.
- Students should be able to identify if something happened in the past, is happening now, or will happen in the future and use the correct verb tense in speaking and writing.

Punctuation

1.5 Punctuate dates, city and state, and titles of books correctly. *(See page 61.)*

1.6 Use commas in dates, locations, and addresses and for items in a series. *(See page 62.)*

Capitalization

1.7 Capitalize geographical names, holidays, historical periods, and special events correctly. *(See page 63.)*

Spelling

1.8 Spell correctly one-syllable words that have blends, contractions, compounds, orthographic patterns (e.g., *qu*, consonant doubling, changing the ending of a word from *-y* to *-ies* when forming the plural), and common homophones (e.g., *hair-hare*). *(See page 64.)*

1.9 Arrange words in alphabetic order. *(See page 65.)*

Listening and Speaking

[**NOTE:** The California content standards for Listening and Speaking skills are listed here so that you can practice them on your own with your student.]

1.0 Listening and Speaking Strategies

Students listen critically and respond appropriately to oral communication. They speak in a manner that guides the listener to understand important ideas by using proper phrasing, pitch, and modulation.

Comprehension

1.1 Retell, paraphrase, and explain what has been said by a speaker.

1.2 Connect and relate prior experiences, insights, and ideas to those of a speaker.

1.3 Respond to questions with appropriate elaboration.

1.4 Identify the musical elements of literary language (e.g., rhymes, repeated sounds, instances of onomatopoeia).

What it means:

Comprehension

● Students should be able to use their own words to recall what a speaker has said, share additional information from personal experiences that relates to the speaker's ideas, and thoroughly answer questions.

Organization and Delivery of Oral Communication

1.5 Organize ideas chronologically or around major points of information.

1.6 Provide a beginning, a middle, and an end, including concrete details that develop a central idea.

1.7 Use clear and specific vocabulary to communicate ideas and establish the tone.

1.8 Clarify and enhance oral presentations through the use of appropriate props (e.g., objects, pictures, charts).

1.9 Read prose and poetry aloud with fluency, rhythm, and pace, using appropriate intonation and vocal patterns to emphasize important passages of the text being read.

Analysis and Evaluation of Oral and Media Communications

1.10 Compare ideas and points of view expressed in broadcast and print media.

1.11 Distinguish between the speaker's opinions and verifiable facts.

2.0 Speaking Applications (Genres and Their Characteristics)

Students deliver brief recitations and oral presentations about familiar experiences or interests that are organized around a coherent thesis statement. Student speaking demonstrates a command of standard American English and the organizational and delivery strategies outlined in Listening and Speaking Standard 1.0. Using the speaking strategies of grade three outlined in Listening and Speaking Standard 1.0, students:

2.1 Make brief narrative presentations:

a. Provide a context for an incident that is the subject of the presentation.

b. Provide insight into why the selected incident is memorable.

c. Include well-chosen details to develop character, setting, and plot.

2.2 Plan and present dramatic interpretations of experiences, stories, poems, or plays with clear diction, pitch, tempo, and tone.

2.3 Make descriptive presentations that use concrete sensory details to set forth and support unified impressions of people, places, things, or experiences.

2.3 Make descriptive presentations that use concrete sensory details to set forth and support unified impressions of people, places, things, or experiences.

Language Conventions

1.1

Sentences

 Clue   First, check to see if the punctuation is missing at the end of the sentence. Next, look for missing punctuation marks within the sentence.

DIRECTIONS: Find the punctuation mark that is needed in the sentence.

1. **How many fish did you catch**
   - (A) ?
   - (B) .
   - (C) ,
   - (D) !

2. **Quick, let's get out of the rain**
   - (F) ?
   - (G) .
   - (H) !
   - (J) ,

3. **What are the answers to 1, 2 and 3?**
   - (A) ?
   - (B) .
   - (C) ,
   - (D) !

4. **The television is too loud**
   - (F) ?
   - (G) .
   - (H) ,
   - (J) !

5. **I asked how much it costs**
   - (A) ,
   - (B) .
   - (C) ?
   - (D) !

DIRECTIONS: Choose the sentence that is correct and complete.

6.
   - (F) Basketball was first thinked up by a teacher.
   - (G) He needed a game for students to play indoors in the winter.
   - (H) He nails a basket to the wall made up a set of rules.
   - (J) I think him had an idea that we all can enjoy!

7.
   - (A) Bird watchers sometimes see birds taking dust baths.
   - (B) The birds use the dust like them bathtub.
   - (C) The dust helps they get rid of tiny bigs in their feathers.
   - (D) The birds is smart to do this.

8.
   - (F) The sunflower can be up to a foot wide.
   - (G) It's petals are yellow.
   - (H) They stem of this flower is very tall.
   - (J) Some sunflowers is twice as tall as children.

9.
   - (F) Find we a map of this town.
   - (G) I think us are lost!
   - (H) We should have turned right on Mason Street.
   - (J) Drive more slower so we can find the street.

STOP

Language Conventions

1.2

Subject and Verb Agreement

DIRECTIONS: Choose the answer that best completes the sentence.

1. Chang and Audrey made _____ kites together.
   - (A) him
   - (B) she
   - (C) they
   - (D) their

2. Are _____ parents coming to the concert?
   - (F) she
   - (G) he
   - (H) her
   - (J) it

3. _____ spoke to my mother on Parents' Night.
   - (A) Him
   - (B) He
   - (C) Us
   - (D) Them

DIRECTIONS: Choose the answer that could replace the underlined word.

4. <u>Tyrone</u> has a baseball card collection.
   - (F) Him
   - (G) He
   - (H) We
   - (J) Them

5. <u>Jill and Keisha</u> went to soccer practice.
   - (A) Him
   - (B) Them
   - (C) They
   - (D) She

6. I thought <u>the play</u> was very good.
   - (F) him
   - (G) her
   - (H) we
   - (J) it

DIRECTIONS: For numbers 7–9, choose the answer that uses an incorrect verb.

7.
   - (A) The skipper steering the boat.
   - (B) The wind blew across the lake.
   - (C) The boat stayed on course.
   - (D) The brave skipper brought the boat safely to shore.

8.
   - (F) The dentist cleaned my teeth.
   - (G) I was worried he might have to use the drill.
   - (H) He were very nice.
   - (J) My teeth are shiny now!

9.
   - (A) The pioneer chose his land carefully.
   - (B) He wanted a stream near his cabin.
   - (C) He wanting good land for crops.
   - (D) He knew he could use the trees for building.

Language Conventions

1.2

Identifying Verb Tenses

Examples:

For Example A and numbers 1–3, choose the answer that best completes the sentence.

A The gift _____ yesterday.

  (A) arrives

  (B) arrived

  (C) arriving

  (D) will arrive

Answer: (B)

For Example B and numbers 4–6, choose the answer that uses an incorrect verb.

B (F) The library have a room for music.

  (G) In the room, you can listen to tapes.

  (H) The room has many music books.

  (J) I love spending time there.

Answer: (F)

---

1. Jeff and Channa _____ us make bread.

  (A) had help

  (B) will help

  (C) helps

  (D) helping

2. Please _____ this letter to the post office.

  (F) took

  (G) has taken

  (H) tooked

  (J) take

3. No one _____ him about the change of plans.

  (A) telled

  (B) told

  (C) tells

  (D) did tell

4. (F) Chang has pick up her heavy backpack.

  (G) She carries that backpack everywhere.

  (H) It has all her art supplies in it.

  (J) She also carries her laptop in the backpack.

5. (A) He forgot to take his jacket home.

  (B) It were a cold day.

  (C) He shivered without his jacket.

  (D) He was very glad to get home at last.

6. (F) Nobody is home today.

  (G) The house is locked up.

  (H) It look strange with the shades down.

  (J) I am not used to seeing it so empty.

STOP

Language Conventions

1.4

Subjects and Verbs

Examples:

For Example A and numbers 1–3, choose the answer that has a mistake.

A   (A) Do you think them will go shopping?

(B) He doesn't like to eat red meat.

(C) His father is going with him.

(D) They will be back soon.

Answer: (A)

For Example B and numbers 4–6, choose the answer that has the simple subject of the sentence underlined.

B   (F) The black bear paced in his cage.

(G) He seemed unhappy.

(H) The noisy children watched him.

(J) Some people like zoos.

Answer: (G)

 Clue   Remember, a simple subject does not include adjectives or any other part of speech.

1.   (A) The dog followed him home.

(B) Him asked if he could keep it.

(C) His parents said that they needed to look for the owner first.

(D) But he could keep the dog if the owner couldn't be found.

2.   (F) They rode through the mud puddles.

(G) Jack and Kim were laughing, and they couldn't stop.

(H) He was covered with mud.

(J) They bikes were muddy, too.

3.   (A) On Saturday, she worked on her hobby.

(B) Her hobby is photography.

(C) Her has taken some good pictures.

(D) We have one that we framed and put in our family room.

4.   (F) My father's next book is being printed.

(G) It is about space travel.

(H) My best friend can't wait to read it.

(J) Dad's first book was a big success.

5.   (A) We aren't ready to leave yet!

(B) My cousin Sally needs to find her umbrella.

(C) My uncle has lost the map!

(D) This trip is a disaster.

6.   (F) You will need yarn, scissors, and paste.

(G) This project is not difficult.

(H) Last Easter, my family made one for our table.

(J) The colorful basket turned out well.

 STOP

Language Conventions

1.5

Punctuation

DIRECTIONS: Choose the answer that shows the correct punctuation.

1. Her birthday is _____ .

- (A) October 16, 1998
- (B) October, 16 1998
- (C) October 16 1998
- (D) October, 16, 1998

2. The movie was filmed on the streets of _____.

- (F) San Francisco California
- (G) San, Francisco, California
- (H) San Francisco, California
- (J) San Francisco: California

3. The new highway will stretch from _____.

- (A) Los Angeles to Sacramento, California
- (B) Los Angeles to, Sacramento California
- (C) Los Angeles, to Sacramento California
- (D) Los, Angeles to Sacramento California

4.

- (F) Lin's family lives in, San Diego California.
- (G) Lin's family lives in San, Diego California.
- (H) Lin's family lives in San, Diego, California.
- (J) Lin's family lives in San Diego, California.

5.

- (A) I sent my package on August 15.
- (B) I sent my package on, August 15.
- (C) I sent my package on August, 15.
- (D) I sent my package, on August 15.

DIRECTIONS: Read the letter. Then choose the answer that shows the correct punctuation for the underlined phrase. Choose "Correct as it is" if the underlined part is correct.

October 12 2003

Dear Akiko,
    Please come to the Fall Festival at Rowndale Elementary School. We will have games, prizes, and lots of snacks! It starts at noon on Saturday.

Very truly Yours
Ms. Michaels

6.

- (F) October, 12 2003
- (G) october 12, 2003
- (H) October 12, 2003
- (J) Correct as it is.

7.

- (A) Very truly yours,
- (B) Very Truly Yours,
- (C) Very Truly yours,
- (D) Correct as it is.

STOP

1.6

Using Commas

DIRECTIONS: Choose the part that does not have correct punctuation. If all the parts are correct, mark "None."

Example:

We had eggs,	toast,	and juice for breakfast.	None
(A)	(B)	(C)	(D)

Answer: D

1. Red, blue, | and green fireworks | lit up the sky. | None
   (A)   (B)   (C)   (D)

2. My friend | lives in | Miami Florida. | None
   (F)   (G)   (H)   (J)

3. Michael's grandmother | was born | on January 1, 1942. | None
   (A)   (B)   (C)   (D)

4. The driver knew | she was a few miles | from Houston Texas. | None
   (F)   (G)   (H)   (J)

5. Main Street School | had its first winter festival | on November 15 1983. | None
   (A)   (B)   (C)   (D)

6. We ate birthday cake | and sang songs | at the party. | None
   (F)   (G)   (H)   (J)

7. (A) Maria Hernandez

    (B) 126 Cherry Hill Road

    (C) Fresno California

    (D) None

Language Conventions
1.7

Capitalization

Examples:

For Example A and numbers 1–4, choose the answer that has a capital letter that is missing. If no capital letters are missing, choose the answer "None."

A Ⓐ I want

Ⓑ to read

Ⓒ The Light in the window.

Ⓓ None

Answer: Ⓒ

For Example B and numbers 5–7, choose the answer that has the correct capitalization.

B The ruler of England at that time was _____.

Ⓕ king George I

Ⓖ King George I

Ⓗ king george I

Ⓙ King george I

Answer: Ⓖ

 Clue   Remember that sentences and proper nouns start with capital letters.

---

1. Ⓐ Oliver knows

Ⓑ he isn't

Ⓒ supposed to do that.

Ⓓ None

2. Ⓕ The theater

Ⓖ is on

Ⓗ Front street.

Ⓙ None

3. Ⓐ did you

Ⓑ find your gift

Ⓒ on the table?

Ⓓ None

4. Ⓕ Tanya lives

Ⓖ on a quiet street

Ⓗ in Chicago, illinois.

Ⓙ None

5. **The bus arrived at _____ more than three hours late.**

Ⓐ the Station

Ⓑ The station

Ⓒ The Station

Ⓓ the station

6. **How was your visit with _____?**

Ⓕ aunt alice

Ⓖ Aunt alice

Ⓗ Aunt Alice

Ⓙ aunt Alice

7. **My uncle lives in _____.**

Ⓐ Paris, france

Ⓑ paris, france

Ⓒ Paris, France

Ⓓ paris, France

STOP

Spelling

Examples:

For Example A and numbers 1–5, find the underlined word that is not spelled correctly.

A (A) <u>identify</u> a bird

(B) bottle of <u>juice</u>

(C) <u>quiet</u> room

(D) All correct

Answer: (D)

For Example B and numbers 6–9, find the word that is spelled correctly and best fits in the blank.

B We opened the _____.

(F) presence

(G) presants

(H) presents

(J) prasents

Answer: (H)

---

1. (A) easy <u>lesson</u>

(B) bright <u>lites</u>

(C) <u>paddle</u> a canoe

(D) All correct

2. (F) good <u>balance</u>

(G) <u>delicious</u> stew

(H) <u>private</u> property

(J) All correct

3. (A) great <u>relief</u>

(B) our <u>mayor</u>

(C) <u>sunnie</u> day

(D) All correct

4. (F) <u>forty</u> years

(G) <u>twelve</u> pears

(H) a <u>thousend</u> questions

(J) All correct

5. (A) my <u>brother</u>

(B) your <u>friend</u>

(C) his <u>uncle</u>

(D) All correct

6. We picked _____ in our garden.

(F) berries

(G) berrys

(H) berrese

(J) berreis

7. The _____ helped me.

(A) nourse

(B) nurce

(C) nirse

(D) nurse

8. The answer to this problem is a _____.

(F) frackshun

(G) fracteon

(H) fraction

(J) fracton

9. Did you _____ the page?

(A) tare

(B) tair

(C) tear

(D) taer

Language Conventions

1.9

Alphabetizing Words

 Clue   If the first letters of two words are the same, move to the second letter.

DIRECTIONS: Choose the best answer.

1. Which of these words comes first in alphabetical order?

- (A) tin
- (B) toy
- (C) table
- (D) trick

2.
- (F) bat
- (G) bear
- (H) bug
- (J) boy

3. Which of these words comes last in alphabetical order?

- (A) cold
- (B) cow
- (C) cream
- (D) clown

4.
- (F) crash
- (G) cream
- (H) cuddle
- (J) comet

5. Which group of words is in correct alphabetical order?

- (A) blue, green, red, yellow
- (B) angry, mad, happy, sad
- (C) apple, cherry, banana, orange
- (D) dance, jump, sit, run

6. Which group of words is in correct alphabetical order?

- (F) giraffe, deer, lion, leppard
- (G) deer, leopard, lion, giraffe
- (H) lion, deer, giraffe, leopard
- (J) deer, giraffe, leopard, lion

7. Which group of words is *not* in correct alphabetical order?

- (A) robin, penguin, stork, wren
- (B) baseball, basketball, football, tennis
- (C) ketchup, mustard, onions, relish
- (D) blouse, pants, shirt, shoes

8. Which group of words is *not* in correct alphabetical order?

- (F) cup, glass, spoon, plate
- (G) breakfast, brunch, dinner, lunch
- (H) orange, peach, pear, plum
- (J) juice, lemonade, milk, water

STOP

Language Conventions

1.0

For pages 57–65

Mini-Test 1

**Written and Oral English
Language Conventions**

DIRECTIONS: Choose the word or phrase that best completes the sentence.

1. Maria is the _____ person I know.

  (A) funny

  (B) more funny

  (C) funnier

  (D) funniest

2. Amelia is the _____ person I have met.

  (F) sincere

  (G) sincerer

  (H) more sincere

  (J) most sincere

3. _____ starting to rain!

  (A) Its

  (B) I'ts

  (C) It's

  (D) Its

DIRECTIONS: Choose the answer that shows the correct punctuation and capitalization.

4. (F) What is your favorite city

  (G) I like San francisco.

  (H) It's in California.

  (J) The golden gate Bridge is in San francisco.

5. (A) October, 12, 2005

  (B) october 12, 2005

  (C) October 12, 2005

  (D) October 12 2005

6. Which word comes last in alphabetical order?

  (F) math

  (G) melt

  (H) monkey

  (J) marble

7. Choose the answer that could replace the underlined word.
Juan built a model rocket.

  (A) Him

  (B) He

  (C) Them

  (D) We

8. Choose the answer that has the simple subject of the sentence underlined.

  (F) The huge circus came to town.

  (G) The funny monkey rode on the elephant.

  (H) Everyone wore beautiful costumes.

  (J) Some people don't like clowns.

9. Choose the sentence that is written correctly.

  (A) Concert in the park last night.

  (B) Music, dancing, and cheering.

  (C) Over a thousand people was there.

  (D) I will never forget that concert.

10. Choose the answer that uses an incorrect verb.

  (F) Our class went on a field trip.

  (G) We collected leaves.

  (H) I gets into poison ivy.

  (J) I won't do that again!

STOP

How Am I Doing?

Mini-Test 1	9–10 answers correct	**Great Job!** Move on to the section test on page 68.
Page 66 **Number Correct**	6–8 answers correct	**You're almost there!** But you still need a little practice. Review practice pages 57–65 before moving on to the section test on page 68.
	0–5 answers correct	**Oops!** Time to review what you have learned and try again. Review the practice section on pages 57–65. Then retake the test on page 66. Now move on to the section test on page 68.

Final Language Conventions Test
for pages 57–66

DIRECTIONS: Choose the answer that shows the correct punctuation mark.

1. How many people were at the party
- (A) .
- (B) ,
- (C) !
- (D) ?

2. Mr. Jefferson was mowing his lawn
- (F) .
- (G) ?
- (H) !
- (J) ,

3. Look out
- (A) .
- (B) ,
- (C) !
- (D) ?

4. Turn right at the stop sign
- (F) .
- (G) ?
- (H) !
- (J) ,

5. Did you get a good grade in math
- (A) .
- (B) ?
- (C) !
- (D) ,

DIRECTIONS: Choose the answer that shows the correct punctuation and capitalization.

6.
- (F) On saturday mornings, we sleep in.
- (G) dad makes pancakes.
- (H) Then we all work on our chores.
- (J) At the end of the day, We rent a movie to watch.

7.
- (A) The bus comes for us at 7:30
- (B) terri likes to ride up front.
- (C) My friends and I like to sit in the back.
- (D) We talk about sports and TV shows?

8.
- (F) the house was dark and still.
- (G) Suddenly, the door creaked open!
- (H) Someone inside the house laughed
- (J) It was my friend, michelle, playing a trick?

9.
- (A) Yesterday, i got a new kitten!
- (B) I have named her tara.
- (C) She came from the animal shelter
- (D) She has green eyes and black fur.

10.
- (F) She and i will study now.
- (G) the library is closed.
- (H) Let's leave now?
- (J) Can I borrow that book when you're done?

GO

11. (A) What is your favorite team?

(B) my dad likes the yankees.

(C) I always cheer for the red Sox.

(D) I cant believe you like the Tigers!

DIRECTIONS: Choose the answer that best completes the sentence.

12. Fred and Janna gave _____ report today.

(F) him

(G) she

(H) them

(J) their

13. Please tell _____ to take this note home.

(A) she

(B) he

(C) her

(D) it

14. _____ called my father on Sunday.

(F) Him

(G) He

(H) Us

(J) Them

DIRECTIONS: Choose the sentence that is written correctly.

15. (A) It was the most small elephant.

(B) First, she climbed onto the tallest platform.

(C) Then the most short clown climbed up, too.

(D) These greater circus performers danced together.

16. (F) I think camping is the funnest thing to do.

(G) We take our biggest tent, the one with the little window.

(H) We find the more quiet campsite we can.

(J) I think our favoriter place is by a little lake in the woods.

17. (A) This is my most better coat.

(B) It is the brightest red that I've ever seen.

(C) It is also more warmer than my other coats.

(D) This more good coat is my favorite.

18. (F) The more emptier house is up for sale.

(G) My most best friend used to live there.

(H) Her mother is the kindest.

(J) I was so saddest to see them move away.

DIRECTIONS: Choose the answer that uses an incorrect verb.

19. (A) The cowboy got on his horse.

(B) He rode quickly away from the cattle.

(C) The lost calf was bleating loudly.

(D) The cowboy taken the calf to its mother.

20. (F) The spider spun a beautiful web.

(G) Dew glistened on it in the morning.

(H) The spider wait to catch a fly.

(J) I'm glad the spider is outside.

GO

21.
(A) The pioneer chose his land carefully.
(B) He wanted a stream near his cabin.
(C) He wanting good land for farming.
(D) He knew he could use the trees for building.

22.
(F) Who wants to go with me to the game?
(G) My sister is a good basketball player.
(H) Her team is in first place.
(J) I would cheering for her team to win.

DIRECTIONS: Choose the answer that shows the correct capitalization and punctuation for the underlined phrases. Choose "Correct as it is" if the underlined part of the sentence is correct.

lena lopez is my best friend. She gave me a great birthday gift. She bought both of us tickets to Bigtop amusement Park. We decided go on Saturday, May 15, after our gymnastics class. We didn't want to go on rides first, so we played some games. I won a teddy bear. Then we ate some cotton candy. We saved the rollercoaster for last!

23.
(A) Lena lopez is my Best Friend.
(B) Lena Lopez is my best friend.
(C) Lena Lopez is my Best friend.
(D) Correct as it is

24.
(F) Bigtop amusement park
(G) bigtop amusement park
(H) Bigtop Amusement Park
(J) Correct as it is

25.
(A) Saturday May 15,
(B) saturday, May 15
(C) Saturday, may, 15
(D) Correct as it is

DIRECTIONS: Choose the word that best completes the sentence.

26. **Don't _____ in the hallway.**
(F) running
(G) ran
(H) run
(J) had run

27. **Please lend _____ your mittens.**
(A) her
(B) she
(C) its
(D) they

28. **Dr. and Mrs. Brown _____ the school last Monday.**
(F) visiting
(G) visit
(H) visits
(J) visited

29. **The vine _____ up the side of the house.**
(A) climbing
(B) climbs
(C) did climbing
(D) climb

DIRECTIONS: Choose the answer that is a correct and complete sentence.

30.
(F) We got six inches of snow last night.
(G) All schools was closed today.
(H) My friends and I builded a snow fort.
(J) We eats our lunch in it.

31.
(A) My family go to the beach on Saturday.
(B) I played in the water with my dad.
(C) A big waves knocked me down.
(D) Ocean water are salty!

32.
(F) My grandmother made a special dinner for me birthday.
(G) I eats chicken, mashed potatoes, and corn.
(H) Then my had cake and ice cream.
(J) My sister gave me a kit to make bracelets.

33.
(A) Last year I start a rock collection.
(B) When I goes to a new place, I look for rocks.
(C) I use my favorite rock to hold my bedroom door open.
(D) I keeps my rocks in boxes.

34. Which group of words is in correct alphabetical order?
(F) apple, ash, all, animal
(G) all, animal, apple, ash
(H) animal, all, apple, as
(J) all, apple, ash, animal

35. Which word would come first in alphabetical order?
(A) drive
(B) do
(C) deliver
(D) dance

36. Which word would come last in alphabetical order?
(F) thermometer
(G) textbook
(H) trail
(J) trunk

DIRECTIONS: Find the word that is spelled incorrectly.

37.
(A) load
(B) October
(C) therteen
(D) myself

38.
(F) weak
(G) harder
(H) yestrday
(J) clown

39.
(A) earth
(B) pudle
(C) broom
(D) packed

40.
(F) sting
(G) heard
(H) messige
(J) pillow

41.
(A) pitcher
(B) rained
(C) softly
(D) dailly

STOP

Language Conventions Test
Answer Sheet

1. (A) (B) (C) (D)
2. (F) (G) (H) (J)
3. (A) (B) (C) (D)
4. (F) (G) (H) (J)
5. (A) (B) (C) (D)
6. (F) (G) (H) (J)
7. (A) (B) (C) (D)
8. (F) (G) (H) (J)
9. (A) (B) (C) (D)
10. (F) (G) (H) (J)

11. (A) (B) (C) (D)
12. (F) (G) (H) (J)
13. (A) (B) (C) (D)
14. (F) (G) (H) (J)
15. (A) (B) (C) (D)
16. (F) (G) (H) (J)
17. (A) (B) (C) (D)
18. (F) (G) (H) (J)
19. (A) (B) (C) (D)
20. (F) (G) (H) (J)

21. (A) (B) (C) (D)
22. (F) (G) (H) (J)
23. (A) (B) (C) (D)
24. (F) (G) (H) (J)
25. (A) (B) (C) (D)
26. (F) (G) (H) (J)
27. (A) (B) (C) (D)
28. (F) (G) (H) (J)
29. (A) (B) (C) (D)
30. (F) (G) (H) (J)

31. (A) (B) (C) (D)
32. (F) (G) (H) (J)
33. (A) (B) (C) (D)
34. (F) (G) (H) (J)
35. (A) (B) (C) (D)
36. (F) (G) (H) (J)
37. (A) (B) (C) (D)
38. (F) (G) (H) (J)
39. (A) (B) (C) (D)
40. (F) (G) (H) (J)

41. (A) (B) (C) (D)

California Mathematics
Content Standards

The mathematics content standards developed by the California State Board of Education are divided into five major sections. The information within those sections tells specifically what your third-grader should know or be able to do.

1) Number Sense

2) Algebra and Functions

3) Measurement and Geometry

4) Statistics, Data Analysis, and Probability

5) Mathematical Reasoning

Mathematics
Table of Contents

Number Sense Standards

1.0 Students understand the place value of whole numbers:

1.1 Count, read, and write whole numbers to 10,000. *(See page 75.)*

1.2 Compare and order whole numbers to 10,000. *(See page 76.)*

1.3 Identify the place value for each digit in numbers to 10,000. *(See page 77.)*

What it means:
- Students should be able to identify place values (ones, tens, hundreds, thousands, and ten thousands) of numbers up to 10,000.

1.4 Round off numbers to 10,000 to the nearest ten, hundred, and thousand. *(See page 78.)*

What it means:
- Students should be able to round numbers by understanding that the place to which the number is being rounded increases by 1 when the digit to the right is 5 or greater (e.g., when rounded to the nearest 10: 485 rounds to 490; 336 rounds to 340). When the digit to the right is less than 5, the number stays the same (e.g., when rounded to the nearest 10: 423 rounds to 420; 954 rounds to 950).

1.5 Use expanded notation to represent numbers (e.g., 3,206 = 3,000 + 200 + 6). *(See page 79.)*

Math
1.1

Number Sense

Using Whole Numbers

Clue — Repeat the questions to yourself as you look at the answers. Think carefully about what you should do.

DIRECTIONS: Choose the best answer.

1. **If you arranged these numbers from least to greatest, which number would be last?**

   1,012   1,022   1,002   1,021

   (A) 1,012
   (B) 1,021
   (C) 1,022
   (D) 1,002

2. **Which of these numbers would come before 157 on a number line?**

   (F) 159
   (G) 147
   (H) 165
   (J) 158

3. **Which of these numbers is nine hundred sixty-four?**

   (A) 9,604
   (B) 946
   (C) 9,640
   (D) 964

4. **Which group of numbers has three odd numbers?**

   (F) 8, 12, 15, 17, 20, 26, 30
   (G) 7, 10, 12, 13, 19, 22, 36
   (H) 2, 5, 8, 14, 18, 28, 32, 40
   (J) 16, 27, 28, 29, 30, 34, 38

5. **Which of these is closest in value to 190?**

   (A) 186
   (B) 192
   (C) 179
   (D) 199

6. **Paul and Vesta used a computer to solve a problem. Which of these is the same as the number on the screen?**

   (F) three thousand one hundred eighty
   (G) three hundred eighty
   (H) three thousand one hundred eight
   (J) three thousand eighteen

7. **Count by fives. Which number comes after 25 and before 35?**

   (A) 50
   (B) 20
   (C) 30
   (D) 40

STOP

Math

Number Sense

1.2 # Comparing and Ordering Numbers

Clue Look for key words, such as "greater than" or "closest," to help you find the answers.

DIRECTIONS: Choose the best answer.

1. You are ninth in line for movie tickets. How many people are ahead of you?
   - (A) 9
   - (B) 7
   - (C) 8
   - (D) 10

2. Which number is greater than 97?
   - (F) 55
   - (G) 102
   - (H) 87
   - (J) 96

3. Which of these is closest in value to 2,000?
   - (A) 1,979
   - (B) 1,997
   - (C) 2,004
   - (D) 2,010

4. What number is missing from the sequence?

   6   12   18   _____   30
   - (F) 20
   - (G) 24
   - (H) 22
   - (J) 26

5. The number 589 is less than _____.
   - (A) 598
   - (B) 579
   - (C) 589
   - (D) 588

6. The number 1,691 is less than _____.
   - (F) 1,609
   - (G) 1,699
   - (H) 1,690
   - (J) 1,600

7. Count by tens. Which number comes after 70 and before 90?
   - (A) 50
   - (B) 60
   - (C) 80
   - (D) 100

8. If a day's snowfall was between 1.01 inches and 2.32 inches, which of the measurements below might be the actual snowfall amount?
   - (F) 1.00 inch
   - (G) 2.23 inches
   - (H) 2.52 inches
   - (J) 2.60 inches

STOP

Math
1.3

Identifying Place Value

Clue — Look at pictures and graphs carefully. When you are not sure of an answer, make your best guess and move on.

DIRECTIONS: Choose the best answer.

1. Find the answer that shows 35 peanuts.

Ⓐ

Ⓑ

Ⓒ

Ⓓ

2. The picture below shows the number of cars parked in a lot. Which answer is the same number as is shown in the picture?

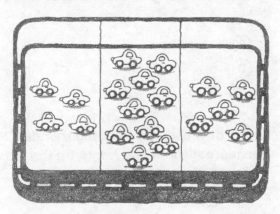

Ⓕ   100 + 40 + 5

Ⓖ   1 + 4 + 5

Ⓗ   400 + 100 + 5

Ⓙ   4 + 10 + 5

3. What number is represented by the chart?

Hundreds	Tens	Ones
I I I	I I I I I	I I I

Ⓐ   335

Ⓑ   533

Ⓒ   353

Ⓓ   335

4. What is another name for 8,488?

Ⓕ   8 thousands, 8 hundreds, 4 tens, 8 ones

Ⓖ   8 thousands, 4 hundreds, 8 tens, 8 ones

Ⓗ   4 thousands, 8 hundreds, 8 tens, 8 ones

Ⓙ   8 thousands, 8 hundreds, 8 tens, 8 ones

5. 8 hundreds and 6 thousands =

Ⓐ   8,600

Ⓑ   8,606

Ⓒ   6,800

Ⓓ   806

STOP

Math
1.4

Rounding Numbers

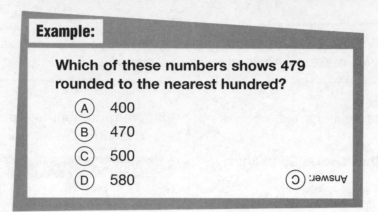

Example:

Which of these numbers shows 479 rounded to the nearest hundred?

(A) 400

(B) 470

(C) 500

(D) 580

Answer: (C)

DIRECTIONS: Choose the best answer.

1. **Round to the nearest hundred.**
   Example: For 350 and up, round to 400.
   For 349 and down, round to 300.

   921 _____ 662 _____ 882 _____

   458 _____ 187 _____ 363 _____

   393 _____ 527 _____ 211 _____

2. **Round to nearest thousand.**
   Example: For 6,500 and up, round to 7,000. For 6,499 and down, round to 6,000.

   2,495 _____ 3,379 _____ 4,289 _____

   7,001 _____ 8,821 _____ 6,213 _____

   5,111 _____ 9,339 _____ 2,985 _____

3. **Round these numbers to the nearest hundred: 575, 612, 499, 633, 590, 680. How many of them will be 600?**

   (A) 3

   (B) 4

   (C) 5

   (D) 6

4. **Which of these numbers shows 587 rounded to the nearest hundred?**

   (F) 580

   (G) 500

   (H) 690

   (J) 600

5. **Round these numbers to the nearest thousand: 1,790, 2,250, 2,120, 1,410, 2,550, 1,490. How many of them will be 2,000?**

   (A) 3

   (B) 4

   (C) 5

   (D) 6

6. **Which of these shows 6,400 rounded to the nearest thousand?**

   (F) 5,000

   (G) 6,000

   (H) 7,000

   (J) 6,500

STOP

Expanded Notation

 Clue Read the questions carefully. Try to think of an answer before you look at the answers.

DIRECTIONS: Choose the best answer.

1. **How can you write 56,890 in expanded notation?**
   - (A) 5 + 6 + 8 + 9 + 0 =
   - (B) 50,000 + 6,000 + 800 + 90 =
   - (C) 56,000 + 8,900 =
   - (D) 0.5 + 0.06 + 0.008 + 0.0009 =

2. **What is another name for 651?**
   - (F) 6 thousands, 5 tens, and 1 one
   - (G) 6 hundreds, 1 tens, and 5 ones
   - (H) 6 tens and 5 ones
   - (J) 6 hundreds, 5 tens, and 1 one

3. **5 hundreds and 7 thousands equals—**
   - (A) 5,700
   - (B) 7,050
   - (C) 570
   - (D) 7,500

4. **What is another name for 8 hundreds, 4 tens, and 3 ones?**
   - (F) 8,430
   - (G) 843
   - (H) 834
   - (J) 8,043

5. **What is another name for 4 hundreds, 6 tens, and 5 ones?**
   - (A) 4,650
   - (B) 465
   - (C) 40,650
   - (D) 4,560

6. **How can you write 9,876 in expanded notation?**
   - (F) 9,800 + 76 + 0
   - (G) 9,800 + 70 + 60
   - (H) 9,000 + 870 + 60
   - (J) 9,000 + 800 + 70 + 6

7. **What number equals 4,000 + 200 + 20 + 2?**
   - (A) 4,202
   - (B) 4,200
   - (C) 4,022
   - (D) 4,222

8. **How many tens are in 60?**
   - (F) 6
   - (G) 10
   - (H) 1
   - (J) 0

STOP

Math

1.0

For pages 75–79

Mini-Test 1

DIRECTIONS: Choose the best answer.

1. If you arranged these numbers from lowest to highest, which would be last?

   1,038   1,084   1,308   1,208   1,803

   (A) 1,803
   (B) 1,208
   (C) 1,084
   (D) 1,308

2. Which of these groups contains all even numbers?

   (F) 2, 8, 15, 24
   (G) 6, 8, 12, 19
   (H) 4, 16, 24, 32
   (J) 10, 13, 16, 18

3. If you round these numbers to the nearest hundred, how many of them would be 300?

   321   233   402   287   430   294

   (A) 2
   (B) 3
   (C) 4
   (D) 6

4. How would you estimate 73 × 48 to the nearest 10?

   (F) 100 × 40
   (G) 100 × 50
   (H) 70 × 50
   (J) 70 × 40

5. How can you write 43,776 in expanded notation?

   (A) 40,000 + 3,000 + 700 + 70 + 6
   (B) 43,000 + 3,700 + 76
   (C) 4 + 3 + 7 + 7 + 6
   (D) 43,000 + 776

6. What is another name for 9 thousands, 5 hundreds, 8 tens, and 8 ones?

   (F) 1,416
   (G) 956
   (H) 9,580
   (J) 9,588

7. Which of these numbers has a 1 in the tens place and a 7 in the ones place?

   (A) 710
   (B) 701
   (C) 517
   (D) 471

8. Look at this number. Increase the value of the number in the hundreds place by 2. What is the new number?

   1,429

   (F) 3,429
   (G) 1,449
   (H) 1,629
   (J) 1,431

STOP

Number Sense Standards

2.0 Students calculate and solve problems involving addition, subtraction, multiplication, and division:

2.1 Find the sum or difference of two whole numbers between 0 and 10,000. *(See page 82.)*

2.2 Memorize to automaticity the multiplication table for numbers between 1 and 10. *(See page 83.)*

2.3 Use the inverse relationship of multiplication and division to compute and check results. *(See page 84.)*

What it means:
- Students should be able to use multiplication to check their answers to division problems (e.g., $6 \div 2 = 3$; $3 \times 2 = 6$). Students should be able to use division to check answers to their multiplication problems (e.g., $4 \times 2 = 8$; $8 \div 2 = 4$).

2.4 Solve simple problems involving multiplication of multidigit numbers by one-digit numbers ($3{,}671 \times 3 =$ _____). *(See page 85.)*

2.5 Solve division problems in which a multidigit number is evenly divided by a one-digit number ($135 \div 5 =$ _____). *(See page 86.)*

2.6 Understand the special properties of 0 and 1 in multiplication and division. *(See page 87.)*

What it means:
- Students should know that any number multiplied or divided by 1 equals that number (e.g., $432 \times 1 = 432$; $432 \div 1 = 432$). Students should know that any number multiplied by 0 equals 0 (e.g., $432 \times 0 = 0$). Students should be aware that dividing a number by 0 is not possible.

2.7 Determine the unit cost when given the total cost and number of units. *(See page 88.)*

2.8 Solve problems that require two or more of the skills mentioned above. *(See page 89.)*

Math

2.1

Addition and Subtraction

 Clue   When you are not sure about a subtraction answer, check it by adding.

DIRECTIONS: Mark the space for the correct answer to each addition and subtraction problem. Choose "None of these" if the right answer is not given.

1. 39 + 21 =
   - (A) 59
   - (B) 61
   - (C) 65
   - (D) None of these

2. 299
   + 54
   - (F) 335
   - (G) 353
   - (H) 355
   - (J) None of these

3. 12 + 29 + 6 =
   - (A) 45
   - (B) 49
   - (C) 47
   - (D) None of these

4. 519
   +56
   - (F) 575
   - (G) 557
   - (H) 577
   - (J) None of these

5. 270
   955
   +116
   - (A) 1,343
   - (B) 1,431
   - (C) 1,340
   - (D) None of these

6. 62
   −17
   - (F) 44
   - (G) 46
   - (H) 45
   - (J) None of these

7. 200
   −80
   - (A) 30
   - (B) 10
   - (C) 20
   - (D) None of these

8. 444 − 44 − 4 =
   - (F) 440
   - (G) 436
   - (H) 410
   - (J) None of these

STOP

Math

2.2

Multiplication

 Clue

Skim the problems and do the easiest ones first. Check your answer by the opposite operation.

DIRECTIONS: Choose the best answer.

1. $6 \times 4 =$
- (A) 18
- (B) 24
- (C) 21
- (D) 32

2. $9 \times 6 =$
- (F) 54
- (G) 49
- (H) 63
- (J) 52

3. $7 \times 8 =$
- (A) 56
- (B) 64
- (C) 63
- (D) 49

4. $5 \times 9 =$
- (F) 40
- (G) 55
- (H) 45
- (J) 42

5. $3 \times 6 =$
- (A) 12
- (B) 15
- (C) 21
- (D) 18

6. $6 \times 8 =$
- (F) 49
- (G) 36
- (H) 48
- (J) 42

7. $10 \times 0 =$
- (A) 10
- (B) 0
- (C) 1
- (D) 11

8. $7 \times 7 =$
- (F) 36
- (G) 42
- (H) 49
- (J) 56

9. $8 \times 9 =$
- (A) 72
- (B) 63
- (C) 81
- (D) 64

10. $4 \times 7 =$
- (F) 21
- (G) 28
- (H) 27
- (J) 32

STOP

Section

2.3 Checking Multiplication and Division

Clue Some problems will be easier to solve if you use scratch paper.

DIRECTIONS: Work the problems. Then draw a line from each multiplication problem to the matching checking problem. The first one is done for you.

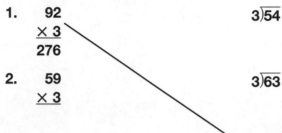

1. 92
    × 3
    276   3)54

2. 59   3)63
    × 3

3. 21   3)276
    × 3

4. 42   3)126
    × 3

5. 18   3)177
    × 3

6. 10   3)174
    × 3

7. 58   3)234
    × 3

8. 28   3)30
    × 3

9. 78   3)84
    × 3

10. 82   3)246
    × 3

STOP

Multiplication

Clue Before working the problem, estimate the answer. Then eliminate answers that are not close to the estimate.

DIRECTIONS: Choose the best answer. Choose "None of these" if the answer is not given.

1. $220 \times 4 =$
   - (A) 880
   - (B) 800
   - (C) 840
   - (D) None of these

2. $3,000 \times 5 =$
   - (F) 5,000
   - (G) 18,000
   - (H) 15,000
   - (J) None of these

3. $410 \times 6 =$
   - (A) 2,466
   - (B) 2,460
   - (C) 2,465
   - (D) None of these

4. $9,000 \times 5 =$
   - (F) 45,000
   - (G) 4,500
   - (H) 36,000
   - (J) None of these

5. $311 \times 22 =$
   - (A) 7,842
   - (B) 5,822
   - (C) 6,842
   - (D) None of these

6. $7,000 \times 7 =$
   - (F) 42,000
   - (G) 56,000
   - (H) 45,000
   - (J) None of these

7. $618 \times 7 =$
   - (A) 4,326
   - (B) 4,426
   - (C) 4,246
   - (D) None of these

8. $999 \times 9 =$
   - (F) 8,991
   - (G) 6,993
   - (H) 7,992
   - (J) None of these

STOP

2.5

Division

 Clue When you are not sure of an answer, check it by multiplying.

DIRECTIONS: Choose the best answer. Choose "None of these" if the answer is not given.

1. 100 ÷ 10 =
   - (A) 10
   - (B) 100
   - (C) 1
   - (D) None of these

2. 426 ÷ 6 =
   - (F) 61
   - (G) 51
   - (H) 71
   - (J) None of these

3. 135 ÷ 5 =
   - (A) 71
   - (B) 17
   - (C) 27
   - (D) None of these

4. 490 ÷ 7 =
   - (F) 70
   - (G) 60
   - (H) 50
   - (J) None of these

5. 880 ÷ 2 =
   - (A) 401
   - (B) 440
   - (C) 400
   - (D) None of these

6. 160 ÷ 8 =
   - (F) 30
   - (G) 24
   - (H) 48
   - (J) None of these

7. 9)189
   - (A) 21
   - (B) 31
   - (C) 41
   - (D) None of these

8. 555 ÷ 5=
   - (F) 11
   - (G) 100
   - (H) 101
   - (J) None of these

9. 200 ÷ 4 =
   - (A) 60
   - (B) 50
   - (C) 45
   - (D) None of these

10. 10)220
   - (F) 22
   - (G) 11
   - (H) 21
   - (J) None of these

STOP

Math
2.6

Properties of *0* and *1*

Mr. 1 Rules

1. **Any number multiplied or divided by 1 equals that number.**

    $4 \times 1 = 4$ $4 \div 1 = 4$

2. **Any number (not zero) divided by itself equals 1.**

    $4 \div 4 = 1$

Mr. 0 Rules

3. **Zero multiplied or divided by any number equals zero.**

    $0 \div 6 = 0$ $6 \times 0 = 0$

4. **Never divide by zero.**

    $7 \div 0$ **not possible**

DIRECTIONS: Write the number of the rule for each multiplication and division problem.

1. **5 × 0**

    Rule _____

2. **4 ÷ 4**

    Rule _____

3. **8 ÷ 1**

    Rule _____

4. **9 ÷ 0**

    Rule _____

5. **3 ÷ 3**

    Rule _____

6. **7 × 1**

    Rule _____

7. **0 ÷ 2**

    Rule _____

8. **6 ÷ 6**

    Rule _____

STOP

Unit Costs

Example:

Shawna has $5.00 to spend on rides at the park. If each ride ticket costs $.50, how many tickets can she buy?

(A) 5

(B) 10

(C) 20

(D) 50

Answer: (B)

Clue   Some problems will be easier if you use scratch paper.

DIRECTIONS: Choose the best answer.

1. If a cake costs $6.00 and 3 friends split the cost equally, how much would each pay?

(A) $1.00

(B) $2.00

(C) $3.00

(D) $4.00

2. Andre has 2 rolls of film. One roll has 12 pictures on it. The other roll has 24 pictures on it. If it costs $0.20 to develop each picture, how much will it cost for Andre to develop both rolls of film?

(F) $2.40

(G) $4.80

(H) $7.20

(J) $6.80

3. Which two things together would cost $30.00?

(A) hat and shirt

(B) belt and socks

(C) shirt and socks

(D) hat and belt

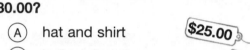
$25.00

$5.00 $18.00 $15.00

4. Mr. Thomas bought 2 adult tickets and 1 child's ticket to the amusement park. How much money did he spend altogether?

(F) $44.85

(G) $29.90

(H) $38.85

(J) $23.90

TICKETS FOR SALE
ADULTS $14.95
CHILDREN $8.95

STOP

Math

2.8

Multi–Step Problems

DIRECTIONS: Choose the best answer.

1. $10 - 1 \div 3 + 3 \times 3 =$
   - (A) 18
   - (B) 16
   - (C) 14
   - (D) 12

2. $1 \times 8 \div 2 + 96 - 100 =$
   - (F) 40
   - (G) 1
   - (H) 12
   - (J) 0

3. $25 \div 5 \times 9 + 75 - 20 =$
   - (A) 118
   - (B) 109
   - (C) 82
   - (D) 100

4. $10 \times 9 + 35 \div 5 =$
   - (F) 30
   - (G) 120
   - (H) 80
   - (J) 25

5. Which sign correctly completes the number sentence?
   $$5 \blacksquare 6 \div 10 = 3$$
   - (A) +
   - (B) −
   - (C) ÷
   - (D) ×

6. Michael has 4 quarters and 2 dimes for bus fare. If the bus ride costs $.75, how much money will he have left?
   - (F) $.25
   - (G) $.35
   - (H) $.45
   - (J) $.50

7. Janna has invited 5 girls and 3 boys to her birthday party. She plans to give each of her guests two balloons and keep one for herself. How many balloons will she need in all?
   - (A) 17
   - (B) 9
   - (C) 8
   - (D) 18

8. Cody played in 3 basketball games. In the first game, he scored 17 points. In the second game, he scored 22 points. In the third game, he scored twice as many points as in his first game. How many points did he score in the third game?
   - (F) 44 points
   - (G) 36 points
   - (H) 34 points
   - (J) 42 points

STOP

Math

2.0

For pages 82–89

Mini-Test 2

DIRECTIONS: Choose the best answer.

1. $26 + 6 =$
   - (A) 30
   - (B) 32
   - (C) 31
   - (D) 20

2. 1,368
   + 5,121
   - (F) 5,489
   - (G) 6,487
   - (H) 6,489
   - (J) 6,589

3. 1,000
   − 275
   - (A) 725
   - (B) 775
   - (C) 825
   - (D) 875

4. 0×21
   - (F) 21
   - (G) 20
   - (H) 1
   - (J) 0

5. 44
   × 4
   - (A) 48
   - (B) 166
   - (C) 176
   - (D) 256

6. **What sign correctly completes the number sentence?**
   $24 \blacksquare 6 = 4$
   - (F) ÷
   - (G) −
   - (H) +
   - (J) ×

7. **What sign correctly completes the number sentence?**
   $72 \blacksquare 9 = 63$
   - (A) ÷
   - (B) −
   - (C) +
   - (D) ×

8. **There are 27 students in a class. Each student brings in 5 insects for a science project. How can you find the number of insects they brought in all together?**
   - (F) add
   - (G) subtract
   - (H) multiply
   - (J) divide

9. **Amir has $3.00 to buy lunch. He chooses a sandwich that costs $1.50 and an orange that costs $.45. How much money does he have left?**
   - (A) $.05
   - (B) $1.05
   - (C) $1.15
   - (D) $1.60

STOP

Number Sense Standards

3.0 Students understand the relationship between whole numbers, simple fractions, and decimals:

3.1 Compare fractions represented by drawings or concrete materials to show equivalency and to add and subtract simple fractions in context (e.g., $\frac{1}{2}$ of a pizza is the same amount as $\frac{2}{4}$ of another pizza that is the same size; show that $\frac{3}{8}$ is larger than $\frac{1}{4}$). *(See page 92.)*

3.2 Add and subtract simple fractions (e.g., determine that $\frac{1}{8} + \frac{3}{8}$ is the same as $\frac{1}{2}$). *(See page 93.)*

3.3 Solve problems involving addition, subtraction, multiplication, and division of money amounts in decimal notation and multiply and divide money amounts in decimal notation by using whole-number multipliers and divisors. *(See page 94.)*

What it means:

- Students should be able to add and subtract money amounts (e.g., $1.25 + $2.50 = $3.75; $10.30 − $8.10 = $2.20).
- Students should be able to multiply and divide money amounts in decimal notation with whole numbers (e.g., $3.20 × 2 = $6.40; $9.60 ÷ 3 = $3.20).

3.4 Know and understand that fractions and decimals are two different representations of the same concept (e.g., 50 cents is $\frac{1}{2}$ of a dollar, 75 cents is $\frac{3}{4}$ of a dollar). *(See page 95.)*

Math
3.1

Equivalent Fractions

Example:

Add missing numbers to make equivalent fractions.

$$\frac{1}{2} = \frac{2}{4}$$

$\frac{1}{2}$ and $\frac{2}{4}$ are equivalent fractions

What does the ■ equal?

$$\frac{2}{4} = \frac{■}{8}$$

(A) 1
(B) 2
(C) 3
(D) 4

Answer: (D)

Clue   Carefully read the numbers and look at the pictures before choosing your answer.

DIRECTIONS: Choose the best answer.

1. $\frac{1}{3} = \frac{■}{6}$

(A) 1
(B) 2
(C) 3
(D) 4

2. $\frac{3}{4} = \frac{■}{8}$

(F) 3
(G) 4
(H) 5
(J) 6

3. $\frac{3}{6} = \frac{■}{2}$

(A) 4
(B) 3
(C) 2
(D) 1

4. **From the figures above, you know that—**

(F) $\frac{1}{3}$ is greater than $\frac{2}{3}$

(G) $\frac{1}{2}$ is greater than $\frac{3}{4}$

(H) $\frac{1}{2}$ is greater than $\frac{1}{4}$

(J) $\frac{3}{4}$ is greater than $\frac{1}{2}$

5. **How much of the circle below is shaded?**

(A) $\frac{5}{6}$

(B) $\frac{2}{3}$

(C) $\frac{1}{2}$

(D) $\frac{1}{6}$

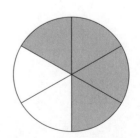

STOP

Math

Number Sense

3.2 # Adding and Subtracting Fractions

 Clue Pay close attention to the operation sign in each question.

DIRECTIONS: Choose the best answer.

1. $\frac{1}{2} = \frac{3}{\blacksquare}$

   What does the ■ equal?

   (A) 2
   (B) 5
   (C) 4
   (D) 6

2. $\frac{2}{8} = \frac{1}{\blacksquare}$

   What does the ■ equal?

   (F) 3
   (G) 5
   (H) 4
   (J) 16

3. $\frac{1}{3} = \frac{2}{\blacksquare}$

   What does the ■ equal?

   (A) 4
   (B) 6
   (C) 5
   (D) 8

4. $\frac{1}{6} + \frac{4}{6} =$

   (F) $\frac{5}{12}$
   (G) $\frac{1}{12}$
   (H) $\frac{5}{6}$
   (J) $\frac{2}{3}$

5. $\frac{7}{9} - \frac{4}{9} =$

   (A) $\frac{3}{9}$
   (B) $\frac{3}{18}$
   (C) $\frac{11}{9}$
   (D) $\frac{11}{18}$

6. $\frac{5}{6} - \frac{4}{6} =$

   (F) $\frac{9}{16}$
   (G) $\frac{1}{6}$
   (H) $\frac{1}{12}$
   (J) $\frac{9}{12}$

7. $\frac{4}{5} + \frac{1}{5} =$

   (A) $1\frac{1}{5}$
   (B) $\frac{5}{10}$
   (C) 1
   (D) $1\frac{4}{5}$

STOP

Section

3.3

Dollars and Cents

 Clue Use a piece of scratch paper to work out problems you cannot solve in your head.

DIRECTIONS: Choose the best answer.

1. **$18.36 + $2.43 =**
   - (A) $21.89
   - (B) $20.79
   - (C) $21.79
   - (D) None of these

2. **$4.64 + $1.46 =**
   - (F) $6.10
   - (G) $5.20
   - (H) $5.15
   - (J) None of these

3. **$10.01 − $0.92 =**
   - (A) $9.90
   - (B) $9.01
   - (C) $9.09
   - (D) None of these

4. **$8.73 − $2.41 =**
   - (F) $6.20
   - (G) $6.22
   - (H) $6.32
   - (J) None of these

5. **$6.00 × $5.00 =**
   - (A) $25.00
   - (B) $35.00
   - (C) $30.00
   - (D) None of these

6. **$20.00 ÷ $4.00 =**
   - (F) $5.00
   - (G) $6.00
   - (H) $4.00
   - (J) None of these

7. **$36.00 ÷ $9.00 =**
   - (A) $5.00
   - (B) $6.00
   - (C) $7.00
   - (D) None of these

8. **A single-scoop ice-cream cone used to cost $1.39. The price has gone up nine cents. How much does it cost now?**
   - (F) $1.42
   - (G) $1.48
   - (H) $1.58
   - (J) $1.30

9. **Notebooks at the school store cost $.75 each. If Hayden wants to buy three notebooks, how much money will he need?**
   - (A) $1.50
   - (B) $2.25
   - (C) $2.75
   - (D) $3.25

STOP

Math **Number Sense**

3.4

Fractions and Decimals

Example:

Which of these is the same as $\frac{7}{100}$?

(A) 0.7

(B) 1.7

(C) 0.17

(D) 0.07   (D) :Answer

Clue   Make a reasonable first guess before you choose your final answer.

DIRECTIONS: Choose the best answer.

1. 0.8 =

(A) $\frac{1}{8}$

(B) $\frac{8}{100}$

(C) $\frac{80}{100}$

(D) $\frac{8}{10}$

2. Which decimal is equal to $\frac{1}{4}$?

(F) 0.25

(G) 0.025

(H) 0.75

(J) .033

3. Which of these is the same as $\frac{43}{100}$?

(A) 4.3

(B) 0.043

(C) 0.43

(D) 43

4. 50 cents =

(F) $\frac{1}{4}$ dollar

(G) $\frac{1}{8}$ dollar

(H) $\frac{1}{2}$ dollar

(J) $\frac{1}{3}$ dollar

5. $\frac{3}{4}$ of a dollar =

(A) 65 cents

(B) 40 cents

(C) 75 cents

(D) 25 cents

6. $1.25 =

(F) $1\frac{1}{4}$ dollars

(G) $1\frac{1}{2}$ dollars

(H) $1\frac{3}{4}$ dollars

(J) $1\frac{2}{3}$ dollars

STOP

Math

Number Sense

| 3.0 |
For pages 92–95

DIRECTIONS: Choose the best answer.

1. $\frac{2}{6} = \frac{1}{\blacksquare}$

   What does the ■ equal?

   (A) 2

   (B) 3

   (C) 4

   (D) 5

2. $\frac{1}{8} + \frac{5}{8} =$

   (F) $\frac{6}{8}$

   (G) $\frac{4}{8}$

   (H) $\frac{3}{8}$

   (J) $\frac{2}{4}$

3. $\frac{7}{16} - \frac{4}{16} =$

   (A) $\frac{1}{2}$

   (B) $\frac{11}{16}$

   (C) $\frac{3}{16}$

   (D) $\frac{4}{16}$

4. **75 cents is the same as**

   (F) $\frac{1}{4}$ of a dollar

   (G) $\frac{1}{2}$ of a dollar

   (H) $\frac{3}{4}$ of a dollar

   (J) $\frac{3}{8}$ of a dollar

5. **Arnell wants to buy 3 books. Each book costs $3.95. How much will he have to pay for all the books?**

   (A) $11.85

   (B) $12.55

   (C) $7.90

   (D) $9.50

6. **Which number is the same as $\frac{22}{100}$?**

   (F) 2.2

   (G) 22

   (H) .022

   (J) .22

7. **Which fraction is the same as 0.7?**

   (A) $\frac{1}{7}$

   (B) $\frac{7}{100}$

   (C) $\frac{70}{100}$

   (D) $\frac{7}{10}$

8.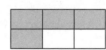

   From the figure above, you know that _____.

   (F) $\frac{4}{3}$ is greater than $\frac{2}{3}$

   (G) $\frac{2}{8}$ is greater than $\frac{4}{8}$

   (H) $\frac{2}{6}$ is greater than $\frac{4}{6}$

   (J) $\frac{4}{6}$ is greater than $\frac{2}{6}$

STOP

96

How Am I Doing?

Mini-Test 1 Page 80 **Number Correct**	**7–8** answers correct	**Great Job!** Move on to the section test on page 98.
	5–6 answers correct	**You're almost there!** But you still need a little practice. Review practice pages 75–79 before moving on to the section test on page 98.
	0-4 answers correct	**Oops!** Time to review what you have learned and try again. Review the practice section on pages 75–79. Then retake the test on page 80. Now move on to the section test on page 98.
Mini-Test 2 Page 90 **Number Correct**	**8–9** answers correct	**Awesome!** Move on to the section test on page 98.
	5–7 answers correct	**You're almost there!** But you still need a little practice. Review practice pages 82–89 before moving on to the section test on page 98.
	0-4 answers correct	**Oops!** Time to review what you have learned and try again. Review the practice section on pages 82–89. Then retake the test on page 90. Now move on to the section test on page 98.
Mini-Test 3 Page 96 **Number Correct**	**7–8** answers correct	**Great Job!** Move on to the section test on page 98.
	5–6 answers correct	**You're almost there!** But you still need a little practice. Review practice pages 92–95 before moving on to the section test on page 98.
	0-4 answers correct	**Oops!** Time to review what you have learned and try again. Review the practice section on pages 92–95. Then retake the test on page 96. Now move on to the section test on page 98.

Name _____ Date _____

Final Number Sense Test
for pages 75—96

DIRECTIONS: Choose the best answer.

1. **Count by fives. What number comes after 45 and before 55?**
   - (A) 40
   - (B) 35
   - (C) 50
   - (D) 60

2. **Which of these numbers is eight thousand, six hundred, and twenty-two?**
   - (F) 8,622
   - (G) 8,602
   - (H) 862
   - (J) 88,622

3. **Which group of numbers has two even numbers?**
   - (A) 1, 2, 3, 4, 5, 7, 9
   - (B) 7, 8, 9, 11, 13, 15
   - (C) 4, 5, 7, 9, 11, 13
   - (D) 3, 7, 8, 9, 11, 15

4. **If you arranged these numbers from lowest to highest, which would be first?**
   3,090 3,990 3,190 3,009 3,999 3,099
   - (F) 3,090
   - (G) 3,099
   - (H) 3,009
   - (J) 3,190

5. **How many tens are in the number 6,792?**
   - (A) 6
   - (B) 7
   - (C) 9
   - (D) 2

6. **Which of these is 1,256 rounded to the nearest hundred?**
   - (F) 1,150
   - (G) 1,200
   - (H) 1,250
   - (J) 1,300

7. **If these numbers are rounded to the nearest thousand how many of them will be 3,000?**
   3,555 3,609 3,432 3,800 3,298 3,626
   - (A) 1
   - (B) 2
   - (C) 3
   - (D) 4

8. **How can you write 26,345 in expanded notation?**
   - (F) 26 + 34 + 5
   - (G) 2,600 + 3,400 + 5
   - (H) 26,000 + 6,000 + 300 + 45 + 1
   - (J) 20,000 + 6,000 + 300 + 40 + 5

9. **What is another name for 3 thousands, 2 hundreds, and 11 ones?**
   - (A) 3,201
   - (B) 3,211
   - (C) 3,210
   - (D) 3,221

10. **6.97**
    + 1.62
    - (F) 8.95
    - (G) 8.59
    - (H) 8.49
    - (J) None of these

11. 270
     955
   + 116

   (A) 1,343
   (B) 1,431
   (C) 1,340
   (D) None of these

12. 12 + 17 + 25 =

   (F) 45
   (G) 55
   (H) 54
   (J) None of these

13. $1.55 + $2.39 =

   (A) $3.99
   (B) $3.49
   (C) $3.93
   (D) None of these

14. $20.09 + $1.18 =

   (F) $21.17
   (G) $20.27
   (H) $21.27
   (J) None of these

15. 7.17
   − 1.62

   (A) 5.45
   (B) 5.57
   (C) 5.55
   (D) None of these

16. 9,550
   −7,010

   (F) 2,450
   (G) 2,540
   (H) 2,550
   (J) None of these

17. 22 − 17 =

   (A) 3
   (B) 4
   (C) 5
   (D) None of these

18. $.39 − $.13 =

   (F) $.20
   (G) $.26
   (H) $.29
   (J) None of these

19. 373
   −369

   (A) 2
   (B) 3
   (C) 4
   (D) None of these

20. 8,661
   −120

   (F) 8,441
   (G) 8,451
   (H) 8,541
   (J) None of these

21. $6.52 − $2.36 =

   (A) $4.14
   (B) $4.15
   (C) $4.16
   (D) None of these

22. 4 × 0 =

   (F) 4
   (G) 1
   (H) 0
   (J) None of these

GO

23. 10
    ×9

   (A) 99

   (B) 19

   (C) 9

   (D) None of these

24. 212
    × 5

   (F) 1,050

   (G) 1,024

   (H) 1,060

   (J) None of these

25. $11 \times \blacksquare = 33$

   (A) 1

   (B) 2

   (C) 3

   (D) None of these

26. $4\overline{)200}$

   (F) 80

   (G) 50

   (H) 40

   (J) None of these

27. $48 \div 6 =$

   (A) 8

   (B) 7

   (C) 9

   (D) None of these

28. $8 \div 8 =$

   (F) 1

   (G) 2

   (H) 3

   (J) None of these

29. $\frac{7}{8} - \frac{6}{8} =$

   (A) $\frac{2}{8}$

   (B) $\frac{1}{4}$

   (C) $\frac{2}{8}$

   (D) None of these

30. $\frac{2}{5} + \frac{1}{5} =$

   (F) $\frac{3}{5}$

   (G) $\frac{4}{5}$

   (H) $\frac{5}{5}$

   (J) None of these

31. $\frac{6}{8} = \frac{3}{\blacksquare}$

What does the ■ equal?

   (A) 2

   (B) 6

   (C) 4

   (D) None of these.

32. $\frac{3}{6} = \frac{1}{\blacksquare}$

What does the ■ equal?

   (F) 3

   (G) 4

   (H) 8

   (J) None of these

33. **Which is the same as $\frac{14}{100}$?**

   (A) 14.00

   (B) .014

   (C) .14

   (D) 1.4

GO

34. Which of these figures shows $\frac{3}{4}$?

35. Which fraction is the same as 0.9?

(A) $\frac{9}{10}$

(B) $\frac{9}{100}$

(C) $\frac{1}{9}$

(D) $\frac{90}{1000}$

36. Which amount is the same as 25 cents?

(F) $\frac{1}{4}$ dollar

(G) $\frac{1}{2}$ dollar

(H) $\frac{2}{3}$ dollar

(J) $\frac{3}{4}$ dollar

37. Which amount is the same as $1.50?

(A) $1\frac{1}{4}$ dollars

(B) $1\frac{1}{3}$ dollars

(C) $1\frac{1}{2}$ dollars

(D) $1\frac{3}{8}$ dollars

STOP

Name _____   Date _____

Number Sense Test
Answer Sheet

1 (A) (B) (C) (D)	21 (A) (B) (C) (D)	
2 (F) (G) (H) (J)	22 (F) (G) (H) (J)	
3 (A) (B) (C) (D)	23 (A) (B) (C) (D)	
4 (F) (G) (H) (J)	24 (F) (G) (H) (J)	
5 (A) (B) (C) (D)	25 (A) (B) (C) (D)	
6 (F) (G) (H) (J)	26 (F) (G) (H) (J)	
7 (A) (B) (C) (D)	27 (A) (B) (C) (D)	
8 (F) (G) (H) (J)	28 (F) (G) (H) (J)	
9 (A) (B) (C) (D)	29 (A) (B) (C) (D)	
10 (F) (G) (H) (J)	30 (F) (G) (H) (J)	

11 (A) (B) (C) (D)	31 (A) (B) (C) (D)	
12 (F) (G) (H) (J)	32 (F) (G) (H) (J)	
13 (A) (B) (C) (D)	33 (A) (B) (C) (D)	
14 (F) (G) (H) (J)	34 (F) (G) (H) (J)	
15 (A) (B) (C) (D)	35 (A) (B) (C) (D)	
16 (F) (G) (H) (J)	36 (F) (G) (H) (J)	
17 (A) (B) (C) (D)	37 (A) (B) (C) (D)	
18 (F) (G) (H) (J)		
19 (A) (B) (C) (D)		
20 (F) (G) (H) (J)		

Algebra and Functions Standards

1.0 Students select appropriate symbols, operations, and properties to represent, describe, simplify, and solve simple number relationships:

1.1 Represent relationships of quantities in the form of mathematical expressions, equations, or inequalities. *(See page 104.)*

What it means:
- Students should be able to use numbers and operation symbols to write mathematical expressions (e.g., $4 + 8$; $9 \div 3$; $10 - 4$).
- Students should be able to write equations, which are mathematical expressions that contain equal signs (e.g., $4 + 8 = 12$; $9 \div 3 = 3$; $10 - 4 = 6$).
- Students should be able to write inequalities, which are mathematical expressions involving one of the symbols $<$, $>$, $\leq$, or $\geq$ (e.g., $8 < 12$; $5 > 1$).
  - $<$ *less than*
  - $>$ *greater than*
  - $\leq$ *less than or equal to*
  - $\geq$ *greater than or equal to*

1.2 Solve problems involving numeric equations or inequalities. *(See page 105.)*

1.3 Select appropriate operational and relational symbols to make an expression true (e.g., if $4 \_\_ 3 = 12$, what operational symbol goes in the blank?). *(See page 106.)*

1.4 Express simple unit conversions in symbolic form (e.g., $\_\_$ inches $= \_\_$ feet $\times$ 12). *(See page 107.)*

1.5 Recognize and use the commutative and associative properties of multiplication (e.g., if $5 \times 7 = 35$, then what is 7×5? and if $5 \times 7 \times 3 = 105$, then what is $7 \times 3 \times 5$?). *(See page 108.)*

Math

1.1

Number Relationships

Clue   Pay close attention to the numbers and pictures in the problems.

DIRECTIONS: Choose the best answer.

1. $\dfrac{2}{3}$ ■ $\dfrac{3}{2}$

   Choose the correct symbol to go in the box.

   (A)   <

   (B)   >

   (C)   =

   (D)   +

2. Look at the number sentences. Find the number that goes in the boxes to make both number sentences true.

   $6 + ■ = 7$

   $7 - ■ = 6$

   (F)   1

   (G)   0

   (H)   13

   (J)   7

3. Which number sentence shows how to find the total number of butterflies?

   (A)   2 + 4

   (B)   4 ÷ 2

   (C)   4 − 2

   (D)   2 × 4

4. Sandy had 5

   She read 2

   Find the number sentence that tells how many books Sandy has left to read.

   (F)   5 + 2 = 7

   (G)   5 − 2 = 3

   (H)   2 + 3 = 5

   (J)   2 − 1 = 1

5. A gardener works for 6 hours and earns $48. Which number sequence shows how to find the amount of money the gardener earns in one hour?

   (A)   6 × $48 = ■

   (B)   8 + ■ = $48

   (C) $48 − ■ = 6

   (D) $48 ÷ 6 = ■

6. A box of popcorn costs $1.25. You pay for it with two dollar bills. How much change will you receive?

   (F) $2.00 ÷ $1.25 = ■

   (G) $1.25 + $2.00 = ■

   (H) $2.00 × $1.25 = ■

   (J) $2.00 − $1.25 = ■

STOP

Name _____   Date _____

Math
1.2

Equations and Inequalities

Example:

3 + 6 + ■ = 10

(A) 1
(B) 2
(C) 3
(D) 4

Answer: (A)

DIRECTIONS: Choose the best answer.

1. 8 × 5 − ■ = 38

(A) 1
(B) 2
(C) 3
(D) 4

2. 12 × ■ = 48

(F) 2
(G) 3
(H) 4
(J) None of these

3. $\frac{1}{4} + \frac{1}{4}$ ■ $\frac{1}{4} + \frac{2}{4}$

(A) <
(B) >
(C) =
(D) None of these

4. 55 − ■ = 23   29 + ■ = 61

Which number completes both number sentences above?

(F) 23
(G) 30
(H) 32
(J) 33

5. $\frac{4}{5} - $ ■ $= \frac{2}{5}$

(A) $\frac{1}{5}$
(B) $\frac{2}{5}$
(C) $\frac{3}{5}$
(D) $\frac{4}{5}$

6.

From the figures above, you know that—

(F) $\frac{1}{4} > \frac{2}{4}$
(G) $\frac{1}{2} > \frac{2}{4}$
(H) $\frac{2}{4} > \frac{1}{4}$
(J) $\frac{3}{4} > \frac{2}{4}$

7. Which number completes this number sentence?

1 + 6 + 7 = 10 + ■

(A) 10
(B) 9
(C) 7
(D) 4

STOP

Math

1.3

Identifying Operation Signs

 Clue If you are not sure of the answer, perform each of the operations until you find the right one.

DIRECTIONS: Choose the best answer.

1. $10 \blacksquare 2 = 20$

   Which operation sign belongs in the box?

   (A) $+$

   (B) $-$

   (C) $\times$

   (D) $\div$

2. $25 \blacksquare 5 = 5$

   Which operation sign belongs in the box?

   (F) $+$

   (G) $-$

   (H) $\times$

   (J) $\div$

3. $18 \blacksquare 9 = 9$

   Which operation sign belongs in the box?

   (A) $+$

   (B) $-$

   (C) $\times$

   (D) $\div$

4. $27 \blacksquare 8 = 19$ $10 \blacksquare 2 = 8$

   Which operation sign belongs in both boxes above?

   (F) $+$

   (G) $-$

   (H) $\times$

   (J) $\div$

5. **Which number sentence shows how to find the total number of feathers?**

   (A) $3 + 4$

   (B) $3 \div 4$

   (C) $4 - 3$

   (D) 4×3

6. **How would you write this operation? Multiply 6 by 2 and add 3.**

   (F) $6 \times 3 + 2$

   (G) $6 \div 2 + 3$

   (H) $6 \times 2 \times 3$

   (J) $6 \times 2 + 3$

7. **How would you write this operation? Add 43 to 46 and divide by 15.**

   (A) $43 + 46 \div 15$

   (B) $15 \div 43 \div 46$

   (C) $43 - 46 \div 15$

   (D) $15 + 43 \div 46$

STOP

Math

1.4

Algebra and Functions

Converting Units

Example:

Which of these statements is not true?

(A) 1 yard = 39 inches

(B) 1 foot = 12 inches

(C) 1 pint = 2 cups

(D) 6 feet = 72 inches

Answer: (A)

Clue Read the problem carefully and determine what information you need to solve it.

DIRECTIONS: Choose the best answer.

1. How many inches are in one yard?

(A) 12

(B) 36

(C) 3

(D) 48

2. How many ounces are in two pounds?

(F) 16

(G) 24

(H) 32

(J) 36

3. How many minutes are in one day?

(A) 24

(B) 60

(C) 720

(D) 1,440

4. A cake bakes for 1 hour and 10 minutes. This is the same as _____.

(F) 60 minutes

(G) 50 minutes

(H) 70 minutes

(J) 80 minutes

5. It takes a plane 4 hours to fly from Ohio to Oregon. This is the same as _____.

(A) 180 minutes

(B) 200 minutes

(C) 240 minutes

(D) 360 minutes

6. Keisha measured the length of a room at 8 feet. How many inches long is the room?

(F) 16 inches

(G) 24 inches

(H) 96 inches

(J) 106 inches

STOP

Math

1.5

Properties of Multiplication

Example:

$12 + 7 = \blacksquare + 12$

- (A) 5
- (B) 19
- (C) 7
- (D) 8

Answer: (C)

 Clue — Work each side of the equation before marking your answers.

DIRECTIONS: Choose the answer that goes in the box.

1. $23 + 16 = 16 + \blacksquare$
- (A) 23
- (B) 8
- (C) 7
- (D) 39

2. If $24 \times (12 \times 12) = 3,456$, what is $(24 \times 12) \times 12$?
- (F) 300
- (G) 3,456
- (H) 1,728
- (J) 576

3. $(10 + 5) + 6 = \blacksquare + (5 + 6)$
- (A) 5
- (B) 21
- (C) 10
- (D) 11

4. $7.5 \times 3.8 = 3.8 \times \blacksquare$
- (F) 2.3
- (G) 8.3
- (H) 7.5
- (J) 5.7

5. $(6 \times 8) \times 5 = 6 \times (8 \times \blacksquare)$
- (A) 45
- (B) 53
- (C) 5
- (D) 48

6. $226 + (835 + 602) = (226 + 835) + \blacksquare$
- (F) 226
- (G) 835
- (H) 602
- (J) 1,663

STOP

Math

1.0

Mini-Test 1

For pages 104–108

1. $\frac{4}{5}$ ■ $\frac{2}{5}$

   Choose the correct symbol to go in the box.

   (A) $<$

   (B) $>$

   (C) $=$

   (D) None of these

2. **Find the number that goes in the boxes to make both number sentences true.**

   $13 - ■ = 5$ $2 \times ■ = 16$

   (F) 3

   (G) 4

   (H) 6

   (J) 8

3. **A case of juice has 24 cans. Each can holds 12 ounces of juice. How many ounces of juice are in the case?**

   (A) $24 \div 12 = ■$

   (B) $24 - 12 = ■$

   (C) $24 \times 12 = ■$

   (D) $■ + 12 = 24$

4. **How many quarts are in a gallon?**

   (F) 2

   (G) 3

   (H) 4

   (J) 8

5. **How many inches are in two yards?**

   (A) 72

   (B) 24

   (C) 32

   (D) 48

6. **Tonya worked on her project for five hours. How many minutes is that?**

   (F) 180

   (G) 240

   (H) 200

   (J) 300

7. **Charles put two quarters and three nickels in a vending machine. How many cents did he put in?**

   (A) 85

   (B) 75

   (C) 65

   (D) 55

8. **Roberta saw a snake at the zoo that was 4 feet long. How many inches long was the snake?**

   (F) 40

   (G) 48

   (H) 4

   (J) 32

9. **If $60 \times 20 = 1,200$, then how much does 20×60 equal?**

   (A) 12,000

   (B) 1,200

   (C) 200

   (D) 1,220

10. **If $10 \times 12 = 120$, then**

    (F) $12 \times 10 = 122$

    (G) $12 \times 10 = 102$

    (H) $12 \times 10 = 120$

    (J) $12 \times 10 = 1,200$

STOP

Algebra and Functions Standards

2.0 Students represent simple functional relationships:

2.1 Solve simple problems involving a functional relationship between two quantities (e.g., find the total cost of multiple items given the cost per unit). *(See page 111.)*

2.2 Extend and recognize a linear pattern by its rules (e.g., the number of legs on a given number of horses may be calculated by counting by 4s or by multiplying the number of horses by 4). *(See page 112.)*

Algebra and Functions

Solving Problems

Examples:

A What is the total cost of 6 gallons of gasoline if 1 gallon costs $1.10?

- (A) $1.16
- (B) $6.06
- (C) $6.60
- (D) None of these

Answer: (C)

B How much juice will it take to fill 10 glasses if each glass holds 8 ounces?

- (F) 10 + 8 = ■
- (G) 10 - 8 = ■
- (H) 10 x 8 = ■
- (J) 10 ÷ 8 = ■

Answer: (H)

 Clue Work the problem on scratch paper, then compare your answer to the choices.

DIRECTIONS: Choose the best answer.

1. Sheri, Amir, and Paolo each bought a snack cake for $.35. How much did they spend altogether for snack cakes?
   - (A) $.38
   - (B) $1.05
   - (C) $1.15
   - (D) $.70

2. Four families each gave $20 to charity. How much money did they give altogether?
   - (F) $24
   - (G) $60
   - (H) $84
   - (J) $80

3. A postal worker walks 16 miles in a day. How far does the worker walk in 6 days?
   - (A) 12 miles
   - (B) 20 miles
   - (C) 96 miles
   - (D) 99 miles

4. There are 24 students in a class. If they form teams of 6 students each, how many teams can they form?
   - (F) 24 − 6 = ■
   - (G) 24 ÷ 6 = ■
   - (H) 24 + 6 = ■
   - (J) 24 + 64 = ■

5. A pet store owner had 18 fish. He had 3 tanks and wanted to put the same number of fish in each tank. How many fish would he put in each tank?
   - (A) 18 + 3 = ■
   - (B) 18 − 3 = ■
   - (C) 18 ÷ 3 = ■
   - (D) 18 × 3 = ■

6. Theresa gets on the bus at 8:05 and arrives at school at 8:20. How long is her bus ride?
   - (F) 5 minutes
   - (G) 15 minutes
   - (H) 20 minutes
   - (J) 60 minutes

STOP

Math

2.2

Solving Problems

Clue   Examine the pictures carefully before you begin solving a problem.

DIRECTIONS: Choose the best answer.

1. **Look at the clock. How long will it take the minute hand to reach the 6?**

   Ⓐ 3 minutes

   Ⓑ 5 minutes

   Ⓒ 12 minutes

   Ⓓ 15 minutes

2. **Which of these is the same as 10 millimeters?**

   Ⓕ 1 meter

   Ⓖ 1 kilometer

   Ⓗ 1 centimeter

   Ⓙ 1 decimeter

3. **If each of these nails is 1.5 centimeters long, how long would they be altogether if you laid them end-to-end?**

   Ⓐ 10 centimeters

   Ⓑ 11 centimeters

   Ⓒ 12 centimeters

   Ⓓ 13 centimeters

4. **A worker at Command Software makes $720 a week. You want to figure out how much he makes an hour. What other piece of information do you need?**

   Ⓕ the number of weeks the worker works each year

   Ⓖ the number of vacation days the worker takes

   Ⓗ how much money the worker makes each day

   Ⓙ how many hours a week the worker works

5. **Which combination of coins makes $.40?**

   Ⓐ 1 nickel, 1 dime, 1 half-dollar

   Ⓑ 2 dimes, 1 nickel, 5 pennies

   Ⓒ 3 dimes, 1 nickel, 1 penny

   Ⓓ 1 nickel, 1 dime, 1 quarter

6. **How many bicycles and cars would you need to have a total of 26 wheels?**

   Ⓕ 6 cars and 1 bicycle

   Ⓖ 5 cars and 2 bicycles

   Ⓗ 4 cars and 3 bicycles

   Ⓙ 2 cars and 7 bicycles

STOP

Mini-Test 2

DIRECTIONS: Choose the best answer.

1. The bridge over a river is 300 feet long. It is made of 5 sections of the same length. How long is each section?

   (A) 45 feet

   (B) 50 feet

   (C) 60 feet

   (D) 65 feet

2. A jogger runs 3 miles every day. How far does she run in one week?

   (F) 15 miles

   (G) 20 miles

   (H) 18 miles

   (J) 21 miles

3. What is the cost of 3 gallons of milk if 1 gallon costs $1.50?

   (A) $1.50

   (B) $3.00

   (C) $3.15

   (D) $4.50

4. A bus has 42 seats. Half the seats are by the window. How many seats in the bus are by the window?

   (F) 21

   (G) 20

   (H) 12

   (J) 6

5. A rancher has 16 calves. He has 4 pens and wants to put the same number of calves in each pen. How many calves would he put in each pen?

   (A) 16 − 4

   (B) 16 + 4

   (C) 16 ÷ 4

   (D) 16 × 4

6. A woodworker wanted to replace the legs on her 6 chairs. How many legs would she have to replace in all?

   (F) 20

   (G) 18

   (H) 25

   (J) 24

7. The third-grade class at Hall Elementary collected gloves to give to a homeless shelter. There are 25 students in the class. Each student collected 1 pair and hung it on a glove tree. How many gloves were on the glove tree?

   (A) 25

   (B) 50

   (C) 100

   (D) 150

STOP

How Am I Doing?

Mini-Test 1	9–10 answers correct	**Great Job!** Move on to the section test on page 115.
Page 109 **Number Correct**	6–8 answers correct	**You're almost there!** But you still need a little practice. Review practice pages 104–108 before moving on to the section test on page 115.
	0–5 answers correct	**Oops!** Time to review what you have learned and try again. Review the practice section on pages 104–108. Then retake the test on page 109. Now move on to the section test on page 115.
Mini-Test 2	7 answers correct	**Awesome!** Move on to the section test on page 115.
Page 113 **Number Correct**	5–6 answers correct	**You're almost there!** But you still need a little practice. Review practice pages 111–112 before moving on to the section test on page 115.
	0–4 answers correct	**Oops!** Time to review what you have learned and try again. Review the practice section on pages 111–112. Then retake the test on page 113. Now move on to the section test on page 115.

Name _____ Date _____

Final Algebra and Functions Test
for pages 104–113

DIRECTIONS: Choose the correct symbol to go in the box.

1. 34 ■ 23
   - (A) >
   - (B) <
   - (C) =
   - (D) None of these

2. 4 + 15 ■ 15 + 4
   - (F) >
   - (G) <
   - (H) =
   - (J) None of these

3. 10 − 2 − 3 ■ 10 + 2 − 4
   - (A) >
   - (B) <
   - (C) =
   - (D) None of these

4. $\frac{3}{5} - \frac{1}{5}$ ■ $\frac{4}{5} - \frac{1}{5}$
   - (F) >
   - (G) <
   - (H) =
   - (J) None of these

5. $3.75 ■ $3\frac{1}{2}$ dollars
   - (A) >
   - (B) <
   - (C) =
   - (D) None of these

6. 4 ■ 6 = 24
   - (F) +
   - (G) −
   - (H) ÷
   - (J) ×

7. 12 ■ 3 = 4
   - (A) +
   - (B) −
   - (C) ÷
   - (D) ×

8. $1.30 ■ $.10 = $1.20
   - (F) +
   - (G) −
   - (H) ÷
   - (J) ×

9. 25 ■ 5 = 5
   - (A) +
   - (B) −
   - (C) ÷
   - (D) ×

10. $\frac{3}{4}$ ■ $\frac{1}{4}$ = 1
   - (F) +
   - (G) −
   - (H) ÷
   - (J) ×

GO

11. 12 − 3 ■ 1 = 10

(A) +

(B) −

(C) ÷

(D) ×

12. 2 × 8 ■ 3 = 13

(F) +

(G) −

(H) ÷

(J) ×

13. 2.4 ■ 1.4 = 1

(A) +

(B) −

(C) ÷

(D) ×

14. $6.75 ■ $.25 = $7.00

(F) +

(G) −

(H) ÷

(J) ×

15. 11 ■ 4 = 44

(A) +

(B) −

(C) ÷

(D) ×

16. A plane has 124 passengers. There are 3 members of the flying crew and 9 cabin attendants. How many people are on the plane?

(F) 136

(G) 135

(H) 133

(J) 112

17. A babysitter works for 4 hours and earns $20. Which number sentence shows how to find the amount of money the babysitter earns in one hour?

(A) 4 × $20 = ■

(B) $5 + ■ = $20

(C) $20 ÷ ■ = $20

(D) 4 × ■ = $20

18. A case of soda has 24 cans. Each can holds 16 ounces of soda. How many ounces of soda are in the case?

(F) 24 ÷ 16 = ■

(G) 24 − 16 = ■

(H) 24 × 16 = ■

(J) ■ + 16 = 24

19. Jackie has 20 yards of rope. She wants to cut it into 5 pieces. How long will each piece of rope be?

(A) 25 yards

(B) 7 yards

(C) 5 yards

(D) 4 yards

20. Delcia earned $200 every week at her job. How much did she earn in 12 weeks?

(F) $1,000

(G) $2,200

(H) $2,000

(J) $2,400

21. The forest service in Red Park planted 25 new trees every year for 4 years. How many trees were planted in all?

(A) 125

(B) 100

(C) 50

(D) 75

GO

116

22. **A student bought a pen and received two dimes and a nickel as change. The pen cost $1.25. How much money did the student give the cashier?**

   (F) $1.50
   (G) $1.25
   (H) $1.00
   (J) $.25

23. **A FleetAir bus holds 30 passengers. FleetAir owns 30 buses. How many passengers can FleetAir seat on all of its buses?**

   (A) 60
   (B) 90
   (C) 690
   (D) 900

24. **Mr. Hoy planted 45 seeds in the fall. He planted 20 tomato seeds, 15 cucumber seeds, and the rest were onion seeds. How many onion seeds were there?**

   (F) 15
   (G) 12
   (H) 10
   (J) 5

25. **Connor saves $3.25 of his allowance every month and puts it in the bank. How much will he have saved in one year?**

   (A) $32.50
   (B) $39.00
   (C) $36.25
   (D) $36.00

26. **The owner of a car factory wants to buy enough tires to use on 143 cars. How many tires will the owner need to buy?**

   (F) 143
   (G) 572
   (H) 366
   (J) 286

27. **It takes a train 36 hours to travel from Boston to Denver. This is the same as _____.**

   (A) half a day
   (B) a day
   (C) a day and a half
   (D) two days

28. **Athletic shoes usually cost $35. The price was reduced by $10. What is the new price of the shoes?**

   (F) $35 + $10
   (G) $10 × $35
   (H) $35 ÷ $10
   (J) $35 − $10

29. **Cara's horse needs a new set of horseshoes every six months. How many horseshoes will she have to store in her barn if she wants to have enough for two years?**

   (A) 8
   (B) 12
   (C) 16
   (D) 24

GO

30. The length of the rug in Geraldo's bedroom is 60 inches. How would he find out the length in feet?

- (F) multiply 60 and 12
- (G) divide 60 by 36
- (H) multiply 60 and 16
- (J) divide 60 by 12

31. Rachel's recipe calls for three pints of milk. There are two cups in one pint. How would Rachel find out how many cups of milk she needs for her recipe?

- (A) $3 \times 1 = 3$
- (B) $3 \times 2 = 6$
- (C) $3 \div 1 = 3$
- (D) $3 + 2 = 5$

32. The level of a pond dropped 72 inches below normal during a dry spell. How many yards did it drop?

- (F) 1
- (G) 2
- (H) 3
- (J) 4

33. Sara has to finish her drawing for art class. She can work on it Saturday morning between 8 and 10:30. She begins at 8 but doesn't finish until 11:15. How many minutes did she work past 10:30?

- (A) 20
- (B) 30
- (C) 45
- (D) 50

34. A recycling company pays 16 cents for each pound of aluminum cans. How much does it pay for each ounce?

- (F) 8 cents
- (G) 2 cents
- (H) 16 cents
- (J) 1 cent

35. Which combination of coins makes $.82?

- (A) 2 quarters, 3 dimes, 1 nickel
- (B) 4 quarters and 2 pennies
- (C) 3 quarters, 1 nickel, and 2 pennies
- (D) 1 quarter, 3 dimes, 1 nickel, and 2 pennies

36. If $a = b$, then $12 \times b = a \times \blacksquare$.

- (F) 12
- (G) b
- (H) 6
- (J) a

37. If $8 \times 2 \times 3 = 48$, then what is $3 \times 8 \times 2$?

- (A) 16
- (B) 24
- (C) 32
- (D) 48

38. $25 - \blacksquare = 19$ $38 + \blacksquare = 44$

Which number completes both number sentences above?

- (F) 18
- (G) 7
- (H) 6
- (J) 14

39. $\dfrac{6}{8} - \blacksquare = \dfrac{2}{8}$

- (A) $\dfrac{1}{8}$
- (B) $\dfrac{2}{8}$
- (C) $\dfrac{3}{8}$
- (D) $\dfrac{4}{8}$

STOP

Algebra and Functions Test
Answer Sheet

1	Ⓐ Ⓑ Ⓒ Ⓓ	21	Ⓐ Ⓑ Ⓒ Ⓓ
2	Ⓕ Ⓖ Ⓗ Ⓙ	22	Ⓕ Ⓖ Ⓗ Ⓙ
3	Ⓐ Ⓑ Ⓒ Ⓓ	23	Ⓐ Ⓑ Ⓒ Ⓓ
4	Ⓕ Ⓖ Ⓗ Ⓙ	24	Ⓕ Ⓖ Ⓗ Ⓙ
5	Ⓐ Ⓑ Ⓒ Ⓓ	25	Ⓐ Ⓑ Ⓒ Ⓓ
6	Ⓕ Ⓖ Ⓗ Ⓙ	26	Ⓕ Ⓖ Ⓗ Ⓙ
7	Ⓐ Ⓑ Ⓒ Ⓓ	27	Ⓐ Ⓑ Ⓒ Ⓓ
8	Ⓕ Ⓖ Ⓗ Ⓙ	28	Ⓕ Ⓖ Ⓗ Ⓙ
9	Ⓐ Ⓑ Ⓒ Ⓓ	29	Ⓐ Ⓑ Ⓒ Ⓓ
10	Ⓕ Ⓖ Ⓗ Ⓙ	30	Ⓕ Ⓖ Ⓗ Ⓙ
11	Ⓐ Ⓑ Ⓒ Ⓓ	31	Ⓐ Ⓑ Ⓒ Ⓓ
12	Ⓕ Ⓖ Ⓗ Ⓙ	32	Ⓕ Ⓖ Ⓗ Ⓙ
13	Ⓐ Ⓑ Ⓒ Ⓓ	33	Ⓐ Ⓑ Ⓒ Ⓓ
14	Ⓕ Ⓖ Ⓗ Ⓙ	34	Ⓕ Ⓖ Ⓗ Ⓙ
15	Ⓐ Ⓑ Ⓒ Ⓓ	35	Ⓐ Ⓑ Ⓒ Ⓓ
16	Ⓕ Ⓖ Ⓗ Ⓙ	36	Ⓕ Ⓖ Ⓗ Ⓙ
17	Ⓐ Ⓑ Ⓒ Ⓓ	37	Ⓐ Ⓑ Ⓒ Ⓓ
18	Ⓕ Ⓖ Ⓗ Ⓙ	38	Ⓕ Ⓖ Ⓗ Ⓙ
19	Ⓐ Ⓑ Ⓒ Ⓓ	39	Ⓐ Ⓑ Ⓒ Ⓓ
20	Ⓕ Ⓖ Ⓗ Ⓙ		

Measurement and Geometry Standards

1.0 Students choose and use appropriate units and measurement tools to quantify the properties of objects:

1.1 Choose the appropriate tools and units (metric and U.S.) and estimate and measure the length, liquid volume, and weight/mass of given objects. *(See page 121.)*

1.2 Estimate or determine the area and volume of solid figures by covering them with squares or by counting the number of cubes that would fill them. *(See page 122.)*

1.3 Find the perimeter of a polygon with integer sides. *(See page 123.)*

What it means:
- A polygon is a closed plane figure formed by three or more line segments joined at their endpoints. Students should be able to find the perimeter of a polygon with integer sides by adding together the lengths of each side.

1.4 Carry out simple unit conversions within a system of measurement (e.g., centimeters and meters, hours and minutes). *(See page 124.)*

Math

1.1

Measuring Objects

DIRECTIONS: Choose the correct answer.

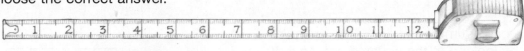

1. **How many inches long is the fish?**

   (A) 5 inches

   (B) 6 inches

   (C) 8 inches

   (D) 12 inches

2. **Look at the paper clip and the pencils. Which pencil is about three inches longer than the paper clip?**

   (F)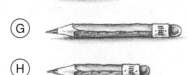

   (G)

   (H)

   (J)

3. **Angela wants to measure a piece of wood. Which of these should she use?**

   (A)   (B)   (C)    (D)

STOP

Math
1.2

Finding Area and Volume

You can estimate the area of an irregular shape by looking at the squares around it. In the example to the right, you know that 4 full squares are covered, so the area will be greater than 4 square units. You also know that the total figure is not larger than 16 square units (4 units × 4 units). You can estimate the area of the figure is between 4 and 16 square units.

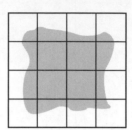

DIRECTIONS: For each of the following figures, estimate the area. Circle the number choice that is most likely the area (in square units) beneath each figure.

1.

3 5 9 2

2.

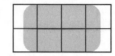

9 8 6 4

3.

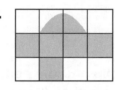

5 6 12 4

DIRECTIONS: *Volume* is the amount of space inside a three-dimensional figure. The volume of 1 cube is 1 cubic unit. Find the number of cubes and volume for each figure below.

4. Number of cubes _____

Volume = _____ cubic units

5. Number of cubes _____

Volume = _____ cubic units

6. Number of cubes _____

Volume = _____ cubic units

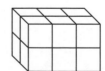

Finding Perimeters

 Clue *Perimeter* is the distance around an area.

DIRECTIONS: Find the perimeter of each figure below. Include the correct units in your answers.

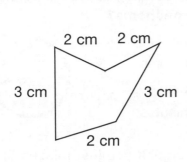

1. _____

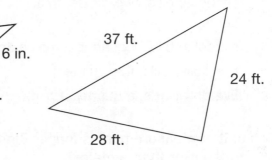

2. _____

3. _____

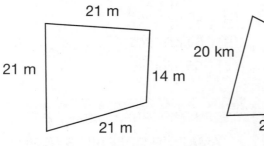

4. _____

5. _____

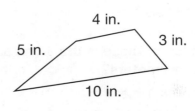

6. _____

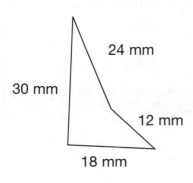

7. _____

8. _____

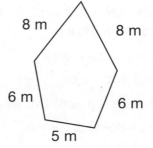

9. _____

Math

1.4

Converting Units

 Clue Pay close attention to the words and numbers in the problem so you know what units the answers should be in.

1. Which answer is the same as $6.28?

- (A) six dollar bills, two dimes, three cents
- (B) six dollar bills, a quarter, three cents
- (C) five dollar bills, five quarters
- (D) five dollar bills, a quarter, a dime

2. Which unit of measurement is longer than a foot but shorter than a meter?

- (F) a yard
- (G) a meter
- (H) a centimeter
- (J) a mile

3. Which of these is the same as 10 millimeters?

- (A) 1 meter
- (B) 1 kilometer
- (C) 1 centimeter
- (D) 1 decimeter

4. After a spring storm, it took 30 hours for the snow to melt. This is _____.

- (F) the same as a week
- (G) about two days
- (H) between one and two days
- (J) the same as a day

5. Rita left dance class at 3:30 P.M. She arrived home at 4:17 P.M. How long did it take Rita to get home?

- (A) 1 hour, 17 minutes
- (B) 47 minutes
- (C) 37 minutes
- (D) 13 minutes

6. Look at the sign. If you just missed the 2:10 show, how many minutes will you need to wait for the next one?

- (F) 50 minutes
- (G) 45 minutes
- (H) 60 minutes
- (J) 55 minutes

AMAZING DOLPHIN SHOW!

Daily at
1:15
2:10
3:05
4:00
4:50

STOP

Math

1.0

For pages 121–124

Mini-Test 1

DIRECTIONS: Choose the best answer.

1. **What would be the best tool to measure weight?**

   (A) a ruler

   (B) a measuring cup

   (C) a scale

   (D) a thermometer

2. **Look at the shaded area in this rectangle. If each square is an inch, what is the area of the shaded part?**

   (F) 289 square inches

   (G) 150 square inches

   (H) 19 square inches

   (J) 10 square inches

3. **A piece of writing paper is $8\frac{1}{2}$ inches by 11 inches. If you wanted to measure a piece of writing paper using the metric system, which unit would you use?**

   (A) meters

   (B) centimeters

   (C) grams

   (D) liters

4. **How many quarts are in two gallons?**

   (F) 4

   (G) 6

   (H) 8

   (J) 10

5. **If the perimeter of this figure is 88 inches, the missing side is _____.**

   (A) 12 inches long

   (B) 20 inches long

   (C) 24 inches long

   (D) 22 inches long

   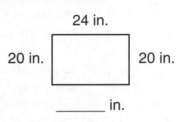

6. **What metric unit is best to use to measure the weight of a large dog?**

   (F) kilometer

   (G) meter

   (H) gram

   (J) kilogram

7. **Elana wants to put a fence around her flower garden. How many feet of fencing will she need?**

   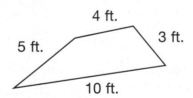

   (A) 22

   (B) 50

   (C) 62

   (D) 33

STOP

Measurement and Geometry Standards

2.0 Students describe and compare the attributes of plane and solid geometric figures and use their understanding to show relationships and solve problems:

2.1 Identify, describe, and classify polygons (including pentagons, hexagons, and octagons). *(See page 127.)*

What it means:
- Students should be able to recognize pentagons (polygons with five sides), hexagons (polygons with six sides), and octagons (polygons with eight sides).

2.2 Identify attributes of triangles (e.g., two equal sides for the isosceles triangle, three equal sides for the equilateral triangle, right angle for the right triangle). *(See page 128.)*

2.3 Identify attributes of quadrilaterals (e.g., parallel sides for the parallelogram, right angles for the rectangle, equal sides and right angles for the square). *(See page 129.)*

2.4 Identify right angles in geometric figures or in appropriate objects and determine whether other angles are greater or less than a right angle. *(See page 130.)*

2.5 Identify, describe, and classify common three-dimensional geometric objects (e.g., cube, rectangular solid, sphere, prism, pyramid, cone, cylinder). *(See page 131.)*

2.6 Identify common solid objects that are the components needed to make a more complex solid object. *(See page 132.)*

Math
2.1

Polygons

Example:

This shape is called a(n) _____.

- (A) pentagon
- (B) hexagon
- (C) octagon
- (D) triangle

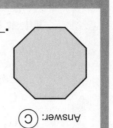

Answer: C

Clue Think of objects, such as stop signs, to help you remember the different shapes.

DIRECTIONS: Choose the best answer.

1. A four-sided figure could be a _____.
- (A) circle
- (B) triangle
- (C) square
- (D) pentagon

2. This shape is called a _____.
- (F) circle
- (G) sphere
- (H) pentagon
- (J) pyramid

3. Which polygon has more sides then a hexagon?
- (A) pentagon
- (B) triangle
- (C) octagon
- (D) square

4. A polygon that has 6 sides and 6 vertices is a _____.
- (F) pentagon
- (G) hexagon
- (H) octagon
- (J) trapezoid

5. What is the perimeter of the polygon?
- (A) 38 inches
- (B) 26 inches
- (C) 28 inches
- (D) 37 inches

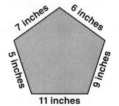

7 inches 6 inches
5 inches 9 inches
11 inches

6. How many sides does a quadrilateral have?
- (F) 3
- (G) 4
- (H) 5
- (J) 6

STOP

Triangles

Example:

What is the perimeter of this triangle?

(A) 13 centimeters

(B) 12 centimeters

(C) 17 centimeters

(D) 18 centimeters

6 cm   3 cm   4 cm

Answer: (A)

Clue If you don't know the meaning of a word, sometimes the answers will give you hints.

DIRECTIONS: Choose the best answer.

1. **A polygon with three sides and three vertices is a _____.**

    (A) square

    (B) triangle

    (C) rectangular prism

    (D) octagon

2. **A triangle with two sides of equal length is _____.**

    (F) an isosceles triangle

    (G) an equilateral triangle

    (H) a scalene triangle

    (J) None of these

3. **A triangle with three sides of equal length is _____.**

    (A) an isosceles triangle

    (B) an equilateral triangle

    (C) a scalene triangle

    (D) None of these

4. **A triangle that has no sides of equal length is _____.**

    (F) an isosceles triangle

    (G) an equilateral triangle

    (H) a scalene triangle

    (J) None of these

5. **Name this type of triangle.**

    (A) equilateral

    (B) scalene

    (C) right

    (D) isosceles

    5 in. 5 in. 5 in.

6. **Name this type of triangle.**

    (F) equilateral

    (G) scalene

    (H) right

    (J) isosceles

    3 in. 2 in. $3\frac{1}{2}$ in.

STOP

Math
2.3

Quadrilaterals

Example:

A quadrilateral with four equal sides is a _____.

(A) rectangle

(B) square

(C) polygon

(D) octagon

Answer: (B)

Clue — Picture each answer in your head before deciding on one.

DIRECTIONS: Choose the best answer.

1. Which of these shapes is a quadrilateral?

(A)

(B)

(C)

(D)

2. Which shape is a rectangle?

(F)

(G)

(H)

(J)

3. How is a square different from a rectangle?

(A) a square has four equal sides

(B) a square has two equal sides

(C) a square has right angles

(D) a square has parallel sides

4. A four-sided figure that has opposite sides that are parallel is called a _____.

(F) pentagon

(G) parallelogram

(H) triangle

(J) hexagon

5. A polygon that only has one pair of parallel sides is a _____.

(A) parallelogram

(B) quadrilateral

(C) hexagon

(D) trapezoid

STOP

Math
2.4

Angles

Example:

An angle that has a square corner
is _____.

- (A) an obtuse angle
- (B) an acute angle
- (C) a right angle
- (D) None of these

Answer: (C)

Clue If you come to a difficult problem, eliminate choices that don't make sense.

DIRECTIONS: Choose the best answer.

1. **What type of angle is less than a right angle?**
   - (A) an obtuse angle
   - (B) an acute angle
   - (C) a right angle
   - (D) None of these

2. **What type of angle is greater than a right angle?**
   - (F) an obtuse angle
   - (G) an acute angle
   - (H) a right angle
   - (J) None of these

3. **Name this type of angle.**
   - (A) obtuse angle
   - (B) acute angle
   - (C) right angle
   - (D) None of these

4. **Name this type of angle.**
   - (F) obtuse angle
   - (G) acute angle
   - (H) right angle
   - (J) None of these

5. **Name this type of angle.**
   - (A) obtuse angle
   - (B) acute angle
   - (C) right angle
   - (D) None of these

6. **Which type of angle has a measurement of 90°?**
   - (F) obtuse angle
   - (G) acute angle
   - (H) right angle
   - (J) None of these

STOP

Three-Dimensional Objects

Example:

A basketball is shaped like a _____.

- (A) pyramid.
- (B) circle.
- (C) sphere.
- (D) rectangle.

Answer: (C)

Clue Imagine what each object looks like before choosing your answer.

DIRECTIONS: Choose the best answer.

1. A cereal box is shaped like a _____.
- (A) pyramid
- (B) sphere
- (C) rectangular prism
- (D) cone

2. An alphabet block is usually shaped like a _____.
- (F) pyramid
- (G) cone
- (H) cylinder
- (J) cube

3. A can of soup is shaped like a _____.
- (A) pyramid
- (B) sphere
- (C) cylinder
- (D) trapezoid

4. What is this shape?
- (F) cone
- (G) sphere
- (H) cylinder
- (J) cube

5. What is this shape?
- (A) cone
- (B) sphere
- (C) cylinder
- (D) cube

6. What is this shape?
- (F) cone
- (G) sphere
- (H) cylinder
- (J) cube

STOP

Math

2.6

Solid Objects

Clue   Decide what the shape looks like before reading the answers.

DIRECTIONS: Many everyday objects contain these shapes. For each object shown below, choose cone, cylinder, sphere, or none of these.

1.   (A)   cone
     (B)   cylinder
     (C)   sphere
     (D)   none of these

2.   (F)   cone
     (G)   cylinder
     (H)   sphere
     (J)   none of these

3.   (A)   cone
     (B)   cylinder
     (C)   sphere
     (D)   none of these

4.   (F)   cone
     (G)   cylinder
     (H)   sphere
     (J)   none of these

5.   (A)   cone
     (B)   cylinder
     (C)   sphere
     (D)   none of these

6.   (F)   cone
     (G)   cylinder
     (H)   sphere
     (J)   none of these

7.   (A)   cone
     (B)   cylinder
     (C)   sphere
     (D)   none of these

8.   (F)   cone
     (G)   cylinder
     (H)   sphere
     (J)   none of these

Name _____   Date _____

Math

2.0

For pages 127–132

Measurement and
Geometry

Mini-Test 2

DIRECTIONS: Choose the best answer.

1. **A pentagon has _____.**
   - Ⓐ 3 sides
   - Ⓑ 4 sides
   - Ⓒ 5 sides
   - Ⓓ 6 sides

2. **What type of triangle is shown?**
   - Ⓕ isosceles
   - Ⓖ equilateral
   - Ⓗ right
   - Ⓙ hexagon

   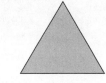

3. **What is the name of this object?**
   - Ⓐ pyramid
   - Ⓑ sphere
   - Ⓒ cylinder
   - Ⓓ cone

4. **Which of these drawings show a right angle?**
   - Ⓕ
   - Ⓖ
   - Ⓗ
   - Ⓙ

5. **What three solid objects have been used to make this object?**

   - Ⓐ sphere, cylinder, rectangular prism
   - Ⓑ cube, cylinder, pyramid
   - Ⓒ pyramid, cylinder, square
   - Ⓓ cone, cylinder, cube

6. **Which of these objects is a cone?**
   - Ⓕ
   - Ⓖ
   - Ⓗ
   - Ⓙ

STOP

How Am I Doing?

Mini-Test 1 Page 125 **Number Correct**	**7** answers correct	**Great Job!** Move on to the section test on page 135.
	5–6 answers correct	**You're almost there!** But you still need a little practice. Review practice pages 121–124 before moving on to the section test on page 135.
	0–4 answers correct	**Oops!** Time to review what you have learned and try again. Review the practice section on pages 121–124. Then retake the test on page 125. Now move on to the section test on page 135.
Mini-Test 2 Page 133 **Number Correct**	**6** answers correct	**Awesome!** Move on to the section test on page 135.
	4–5 answers correct	**You're almost there!** But you still need a little practice. Review practice pages 127–132 before moving on to the section test on page 135.
	0–3 answers correct	**Oops!** Time to review what you have learned and try again. Review the practice section on pages 127–132. Then retake the test on page 133. Now move on to the section test on page 135.

Name _____   Date _____

Final Measurement and Geometry Test
for pages 121–133

DIRECTIONS: Choose the best answer.

1. A four-sided figure could be a _____.
   - (A) circle
   - (B) triangle
   - (C) square
   - (D) pentagon

2. This shape is called a _____.
   - (F) hexagon
   - (G) pentagon
   - (H) octagon
   - (J) pyramid

3. What time does the clock show?
   - (A) 9:45
   - (B) 10:15
   - (C) 10:45
   - (D) 11:00

4. Which of these statements is not true?
   - (F) 12 inches = 1 foot
   - (G) 16 ounces = 1 pound
   - (H) 4 feet = 1 yard
   - (J) 4 quarts = 1 gallon

5. What is the temperature shown on the thermometer?
   - (A) 74°
   - (B) 66°
   - (C) 64°
   - (D) 54°

6. If you wanted to measure the length of a football field, what unit would you most likely use?
   - (F) inches
   - (G) centimeters
   - (H) yards
   - (J) miles

7. The perimeter of this figure is _____.
   - (A) 12 units
   - (B) 20 units
   - (C) 14 units
   - (D) not enough information

8. Which of these objects is shaped like a cube?
   - (F)
   - (G)
   - (H)
   - (J)

GO

Name _____ Date _____

9. This shape is called a _____.

  (A) cube
  (B) sphere
  (C) cylinder
  (D) pyramid

---

10. Which of these shapes can be folded along the dotted line so the parts match?

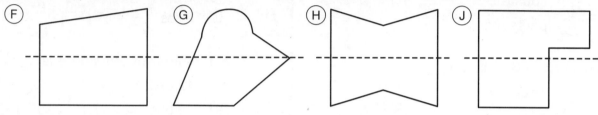

---

11. Which statement about this pattern is true?

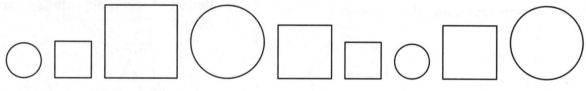

  (A) There are more circles than squares
  (B) There are the same number of squares and circles.
  (C) The smallest circle is always beside the largest square.
  (D) The smallest circle is always beside the smallest square.

---

12. If you cut a sphere in half, which of these would be formed?

13. Which angle is less than a right angle?

(A)

(B)

(C)

(D)

14. What type of angle is this?

(F) obtuse angle
(G) acute angle
(H) right angle
(J) none of these

15. What type of angle is this?

(A) obtuse angle
(B) acute angle
(C) right angle
(D) none of these

16. What type of angle is this?

(F) obtuse angle
(G) acute angle
(H) right angle
(J) none of these

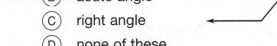

17. Which triangle is an isosceles triangle?

(A)
(B)
(C)
(D)

18. Which triangle is an equilateral triangle?

(F)
(G)
(H)
(J)

19. Which of these shapes has one more side than a square?

(A)

(B)

(C)

(D)

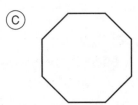
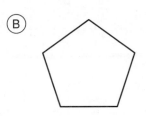
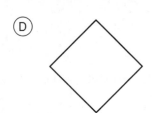

GO

20. Bonnie folded a piece of paper in half and then folded it in half again. The picture shows how she folded her paper. What will the piece of paper look like when Bonnie unfolds it?

(F) 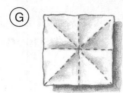 (G) 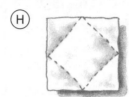 (H)  (J)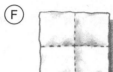

---

21. Coach Garcia wants to measure the speed of two runners. Which of these should she use?

(A)

(B)

(C)

(D)

STOP

Measurement and Geometry Test
Answer Sheet

1 Ⓐ Ⓑ Ⓒ Ⓓ
2 Ⓕ Ⓖ Ⓗ Ⓙ
3 Ⓐ Ⓑ Ⓒ Ⓓ
4 Ⓕ Ⓖ Ⓗ Ⓙ
5 Ⓐ Ⓑ Ⓒ Ⓓ
6 Ⓕ Ⓖ Ⓗ Ⓙ
7 Ⓐ Ⓑ Ⓒ Ⓓ
8 Ⓕ Ⓖ Ⓗ Ⓙ
9 Ⓐ Ⓑ Ⓒ Ⓓ
10 Ⓕ Ⓖ Ⓗ Ⓙ

11 Ⓐ Ⓑ Ⓒ Ⓓ
12 Ⓕ Ⓖ Ⓗ Ⓙ
13 Ⓐ Ⓑ Ⓒ Ⓓ
14 Ⓕ Ⓖ Ⓗ Ⓙ
15 Ⓐ Ⓑ Ⓒ Ⓓ
16 Ⓕ Ⓖ Ⓗ Ⓙ
17 Ⓐ Ⓑ Ⓒ Ⓓ
18 Ⓕ Ⓖ Ⓗ Ⓙ
19 Ⓐ Ⓑ Ⓒ Ⓓ
20 Ⓕ Ⓖ Ⓗ Ⓙ

21 Ⓐ Ⓑ Ⓒ Ⓓ

Statistics, Data Analysis, and Probability Standards

1.0 Students conduct simple probability experiments by determining the number of possible outcomes and make simple predictions:

1.1 Identify whether common events are certain, likely, unlikely, or improbable. *(See page 141.)*

1.2 Record the possible outcomes for a simple event (e.g., tossing a coin) and systematically keep track of the outcomes when the event is repeated many times. *(See page 142.)*

1.3 Summarize and display the results of probability experiments in a clear and organized way (e.g., use a bar graph or a line plot). *(See page 143.)*

1.4 Use the results of probability experiments to predict future events (e.g., use a line plot to predict the temperature forecast for the next day). *(See page 144.)*

Name _____   Date _____

Math

Determining Likelihood

Clue   Review the numbers and colors of each button as you read the answers.

DIRECTIONS: Choose the best answer.

Melanie put 3 yellow buttons, 6 red buttons, 2 blue buttons, and 1 green button in a bag. Mikel draws one button out of the bag each time. Answer the questions below.

1. What is the chance that Mikel will pull out a yellow button?

- (A) 3 out of 12
- (B) 4 out of 12
- (C) 1 out of 12
- (D) 6 out of 12

2. What is the chance that Mikel will pull out a blue button?

- (F) 1 out of 12
- (G) 4 out of 12
- (H) 5 out of 12
- (J) 2 out of 12

3. What is the chance that Mikel will pull out a red button?

- (A) 4 out of 12
- (B) 6 out of 12
- (C) 3 out of 12
- (D) 2 out of 12

4. What is the chance that Mikel will pull out a green button?

- (F) 2 out of 12
- (G) 4 out of 12
- (H) 1 out of 12
- (J) 6 out of 12

5. Which color is Mikel most likely to pull out?

- (A) yellow
- (B) blue
- (C) red
- (D) green

6. Which color is Mikel least likely to pull out?

- (F) yellow
- (G) blue
- (H) red
- (J) green

7. What should Melanie do if she wants to have an equal chance of getting a blue button and a green button?

- (A) add 1 green button
- (B) remove 1 red button
- (C) add 1 blue button
- (D) remove 1 green button

STOP

Math

1.2

Tracking Outcomes

 Clue Make sure you understand the chart before moving on to the questions.

DIRECTIONS: Choose the best answer.

Kim used 3 pennies to do an experiment. She flipped the coins together 8 different times. The chart below shows how often she got heads (H) and how often she got tails (T). Look at the chart and answer the questions.

	Coin 1	Coin 2	Coin 3
Flip 1	H	H	H
Flip 2	H	T	H
Flip 3	H	T	T
Flip 4	H	H	T
Flip 5	T	T	T
Flip 6	T	H	T
Flip 7	T	H	H
Flip 8	T	T	H

1. **After flipping the coins 8 times, how many times did Kim get heads?**
   - (A) 6
   - (B) 10
   - (C) 12
   - (D) 14

2. **After flipping the coins 8 times, how many times did Kim get tails?**
   - (F) 6
   - (G) 10
   - (H) 12
   - (J) 14

3. **How many times did she get exactly 2 heads in one flip?**
   - (A) 7
   - (B) 4
   - (C) 5
   - (D) 3

4. **How many times did she get 3 tails in one flip?**
   - (F) 4
   - (G) 1
   - (H) 3
   - (J) 2

5. **How many times did she get 2 or more heads in one flip?**
   - (A) 4
   - (B) 3
   - (C) 5
   - (D) 1

6. **What were Kim's chances of getting heads on one flip of one coin?**
   - (F) 1 out of 3
   - (G) 1 out of 2
   - (H) 1 out of 8
   - (J) 1 out of 18

STOP

Math
1.3

Plotting Outcomes

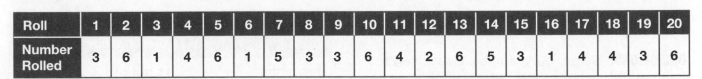

Roll	1	2	3	4	5	6	7	8	9	10	11	12	13	14	15	16	17	18	19	20
Number Rolled	3	6	1	4	6	1	5	3	3	6	4	2	6	5	3	1	4	4	3	6

DIRECTIONS: A student rolled a 6-sided number cube 20 times. The results are shown in the table above. Read the table and then use the information to fill in the line graph. Then answer the questions.

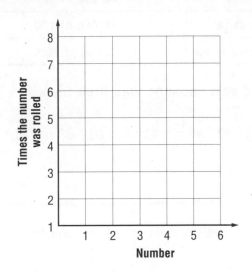

1. How many times did the student roll a 4?

- (A) 2
- (B) 3
- (C) 4
- (D) 5

2. What number did he roll the least?

- (F) 1
- (G) 2
- (H) 3
- (J) 6

3. How many times did he roll an even number?

- (A) 10
- (B) 12
- (C) 13
- (D) 14

4. How many times did he roll an odd number?

- (F) 13
- (G) 14
- (H) 10
- (J) 16

5. What two numbers came up the most?

- (A) 2, 5
- (B) 1, 2
- (C) 1, 5
- (D) 3, 6

STOP

Math

1.4

Making Predictions

Statistics, Data Analysis,
and Probability

DIRECTIONS: Gerard did a survey. He wanted to find out what topping third-graders like most on their pizza. He asked 100 students to name their favorite topping. His results are in the table. Read the results and answer the questions.

Topping	Number of students who said this was their favorite topping
pepperoni	11 out of 100
onions	5 out of 100
cheese	68 out of 100
sausage	10 out of 100
mushrooms	2 out of 100

1. **Based on Gerard's results, how many third-graders said sausage was their favorite topping?**

   (A) 2 out of 100   (B) 11 out of 100   (C) 10 out of 100   (D) 68 out of 100

2. **What topping did students like the least?**

   (F) pepperoni   (G) cheese   (H) mushrooms   (J) onions

3. **Which bar graph shows Gerard's results correctly?**

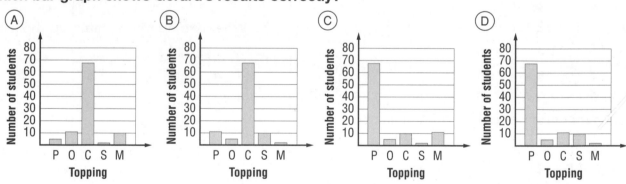

4. **If you surveyed the third-graders in your school, what topping do you predict would be their favorite? Make your prediction based on Gerard's survey.**

   (F) pepperoni

   (G) sausage

   (H) cheese

   (J) mushrooms

STOP

Name _____   Date _____

Math

1.0

For pages 141–144

Mini-Test 1

Statistics, Data Analysis,
and Probability

DIRECTIONS: Use the spinner to answer the questions.

Spinner 1   Spinner 2

1. **How many different objects are on Spinner 1?**
   - (A) 1
   - (B) 2
   - (C) 3
   - (D) 4

2. **What are the chances of spinning a square on Spinner 1?**
   - (F) 0 out of 4
   - (G) 1 out of 4
   - (H) 2 out of 4
   - (J) 3 out of 4

3. **What are the chances of spinning a circle on Spinner 1?**
   - (A) 1 out of 4
   - (B) 2 out of 4
   - (C) 3 out of 4
   - (D) 4 out of 4

4. **How many different objects are on Spinner 2?**
   - (F) 2
   - (G) 4
   - (H) 6
   - (J) 8

5. **Into how many sections is Spinner 2 divided?**
   - (A) 2
   - (B) 4
   - (C) 6
   - (D) 8

6. **How many stars are on Spinner 2?**
   - (F) 2
   - (G) 3
   - (H) 4
   - (J) 1

7. **What are the chances of spinning a star on Spinner 2?**
   - (A) 3 out of 4
   - (B) 2 out of 8
   - (C) 3 out of 4
   - (D) 3 out of 8

8. **What are the chances of spinning a square on Spinner 2?**
   - (F) 2 out of 8
   - (G) 3 out of 8
   - (H) 1 out of 8
   - (J) 4 out of 8

9. **Which object are you least likely to spin on Spinner 2?**
   - (A) circle
   - (B) star
   - (C) triangle
   - (D) square

STOP

How Am I Doing?

Mini-Test 1	8–9 answers correct	**Great Job!** Move on to the section test on page 147.
Page 145	5–7 answers correct	**You're almost there!** But you still need a little practice. Review practice pages 141–144 before moving on to the section test on page 147.
Number Correct	0–4 answers correct	**Oops!** Time to review what you have learned and try again. Review the practice section on pages 141–144. Then retake the test on page 145. Now move on to the section test on page 147.

Final Statistics, Data Analysis, and Probability Test
for pages 141–145

1. The children in the Chang family were stuck inside on a rainy day. They decided to make their own games. They each made a spinner. When Jennie spun her spinner, the color it landed on was gray. Which spinner was probably Jennie's?

   Ⓐ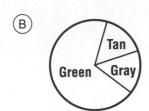

   Ⓑ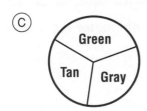

   Ⓒ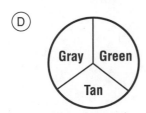

   Ⓓ

2. If you use this spinner, what are your chances of landing on a star?

   Ⓕ 1 in 2
   Ⓖ 1 in 3
   Ⓗ 2 in 4
   Ⓙ 1 in 5

3. Ryan flipped a coin. What are the chances that it will come up tails?

   Ⓐ 0
   Ⓑ 1 in 1
   Ⓒ 1 in 2
   Ⓓ 2 in 2

4. Maya flipped two coins at the same time. What are the chances that both will come up heads?

   Ⓕ 1 in 2
   Ⓖ 1 in 3
   Ⓗ 1 in 4
   Ⓙ 1 in 6

DIRECTIONS: Use the graph to answer numbers 5–8.

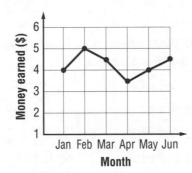

5. The line graph shows how much money Sara earned each month by helping around the house. How much money did she earn in April?

   Ⓐ $3.50
   Ⓑ $4.00
   Ⓒ $4.50
   Ⓓ $5.00

GO

6. In which month did she earn the most?

(F) January

(G) February

(H) March

(J) June

7. How much money did she earn in all?

(A) $24.50

(B) $25.00

(C) $25.50

(D) $26.00

8. Based on what Sara earned for the first 6 months of this year, how likely is it that she will earn more than $100 in the last 6 months of this year?

(F) very likely

(G) likely

(H) unlikely

(J) very unlikely

9. What are your chances of spinning a triangle on this spinner?

(A) 2 out of 8

(B) 3 out of 3

(C) 2 out of 3

(D) 1 out of 8

10. Which object are you most likely to spin on the spinner above?

(F) star

(G) triangle

(H) circle

(J) square

DIRECTIONS: Brad put 4 green jelly beans, 5 red jelly beans, 2 yellow jelly beans, and 1 purple jelly bean in a jar. His sister closed her eyes and pulled out one at a time.

11. What is the chance that his sister will pull out a yellow jelly bean?

(A) 2 out of 12

(B) 2 out of 2

(C) 3 out of 8

(D) 2 out of 10

12. Which color will his sister most likely pull out?

(F) green

(G) red

(H) yellow

(J) purple

13. Which color will his sister least likely pull out?

(A) green

(B) red

(C) yellow

(D) purple

STOP

Name _____   Date _____

Final Statistics, Data Analysis, and Probability Test

Answer Sheet

1. (A) (B) (C) (D)
2. (F) (G) (H) (J)
3. (A) (B) (C) (D)
4. (F) (G) (H) (J)
5. (A) (B) (C) (D)
6. (F) (G) (H) (J)
7. (A) (B) (C) (D)
8. (F) (G) (H) (J)
9. (A) (B) (C) (D)
10. (F) (G) (H) (J)
11. (A) (B) (C) (D)
12. (F) (G) (H) (J)
13. (A) (B) (C) (D)

Mathematical Reasoning Standards

1.0 Students make decisions about how to approach problems:

1.1 Analyze problems by identifying relationships, distinguishing relevant from irrelevant information, sequencing and prioritizing information, and observing patterns. *(See page 151.)*

What it means:

- When presented with a math problem, students should be able to gather the correct information, in the correct order, and apply relevant mathematical concepts. For example, given the problem: *Seven white ducks, four brown geese, and one black dog are swimming in the pond. What is the difference in the number of ducks and geese?*

- Students should determine that they will need to use subtraction to find the answer, that irrelevant information includes the colors mentioned and the dog, and that they will need to subtract the smaller number (geese) from the larger number (ducks).

1.2 Determine when and how to break a problem into simpler parts. *(See page 152.)*

What it means:

- Given the problem: *Your teacher is looking for a place to put the gerbil cage for the afternoon. The cage is $2\frac{1}{2}$ feet long. Your desk is 3 feet long. Your books take up 1 foot of space on your desk. Do you have room on your desk for the cage?*

- Students should be able to break down the problem by first determining how much room they have available on their desk (3 feet - 1 foot = 2 feet). Then they should be able to compare the available space (2 feet) to the needed space ($2\frac{1}{2}$ feet) and realize there is not enough room for the cage.

Math

Mathematical Reasoning

Analyzing Problems

1.1

> **Clue** Break each problem into parts to help you understand it.

DIRECTIONS: Choose the best answer.

1. Jennie had three bent nails in her pocket. Then she put five straight nails in her pocket. Which answer shows what she had in her pocket?

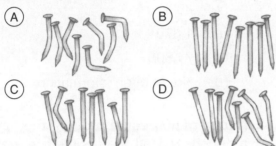

Ⓐ   Ⓑ

Ⓒ   Ⓓ

2. Tai carried 4 boxes of tiles into the kitchen. Each box held 12 tiles. What would you do to find out how many tiles he carried into the kitchen all together?

Ⓕ multiply

Ⓖ subtract

Ⓗ divide

Ⓙ None of these

3. Which of these is most likely measured in feet?

Ⓐ the distance around a room

Ⓑ the weight of a large box

Ⓒ the distance to the moon

Ⓓ the amount of water in a pool

4. This map shows Janelle's yard. She came in through the gate and walked east for 3 yards. Then she went north for 2 yards. What was she closest to?

Ⓕ the swing

Ⓖ the pond

Ⓗ the steps

Ⓙ the garden

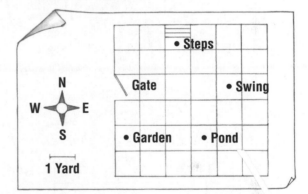

5. Rick is carving a pattern in a piece of wood. Which shapes are missing from the pattern?

 Ⓐ   Ⓑ   Ⓒ   Ⓓ

STOP

Math

1.2

Breaking Problems into Parts

Clue   Use scratch paper to help you remember steps and numbers in each problem.

DIRECTIONS: Choose the best answer.

1. Look at the graph below and the report Willie made about the coins in his change jar. How many dimes did Willie have in the change jar?

   (A) 7

   (B) 11

   (C) 18

   (D) 6

Willie's Report
I had more pennies than any other coin. There were the fewest nickels. I had more dimes than quarters.

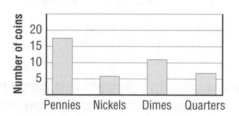

Number of coins

Pennies   Nickels   Dimes   Quarters

2. Michael was at a card convention. At the first booth he bought 8 cards. He bought 6 cards at each of the remaining 9 booths. How many cards did Michael buy altogether?

   (F) 54 cards

   (G) 62 cards

   (H) 57 cards

   (J) 72 cards

3. There were 85 boxes shipped to the warehouse. In each box there were 22 cartons. In each carton there were 40 water guns. How many water guns are in all 85 boxes?

   (A) 880

   (B) 1,870

   (C) 74,800

   (D) Not enough information

4. A total of 60 people brought their pets to a pet show. Half the people brought dogs and 20 people brought cats. How many people brought other kinds of pets?

   (F) 30

   (G) 10

   (H) 20

   (J) 40

5. A doctor has her office open 5 days a week, 8 hours a day. If she sees 4 patients an hour, how many patients does she see in 1 day?

   (A) 24

   (B) 28

   (C) 38

   (D) 32

STOP

Math

Mathematical Reasoning

1.0

Mini-Test 1

For pages 151–152

DIRECTIONS: The third grade students at Millbrook School made a graph about where they wanted to go on vacation. Study the graph, then do numbers 1–3.

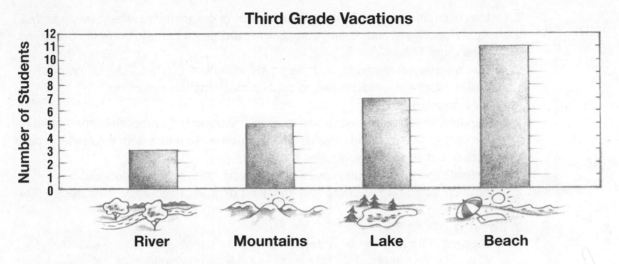

Third Grade Vacations

1. **Which of these is another way to show how many students went to the beach?**

   Ⓐ THL THL I

   Ⓑ THL I

   Ⓒ THL THL

   Ⓓ THL THL IIII

2. **How many students went to a lake for vacation?**

   Ⓕ 11

   Ⓖ 7

   Ⓗ 8

   Ⓙ 5

3. **Two of the students changed their minds and decided to go to a lake instead of the beach. How many students then wanted to go to a lake?**

   Ⓐ 7

   Ⓑ 8

   Ⓒ 5

   Ⓓ 9

STOP

Mathematical Reasoning Standards

2.0 Students use strategies, skills, and concepts in finding solutions:

2.1 Use estimation to verify the reasonableness of calculated results. *(See page 155.)*

2.2 Apply strategies and results from simpler problems to more complex problems. *(See page 156.)*

2.3 Use a variety of methods, such as words, numbers, symbols, charts, graphs, tables, diagrams, and models, to explain mathematical reasoning. *(See page 157.)*

2.4 Express the solution clearly and logically by using the appropriate mathematical notation and terms and clear language; support solutions with evidence in both verbal and symbolic work. *(See page 158.)*

2.5 Indicate the relative advantages of exact and approximate solutions to problems and give answers to a specified degree of accuracy. *(See page 159.)*

What it means:
- Students should be able to determine when estimates are acceptable (e.g., The lake is about 25 feet deep.), and when accurate information is necessary (e.g., The recipe calls for 1 cup of sugar.)

2.6 Make precise calculations and check the validity of the results from the context of the problem. *(See page 160.)*

3.0 Students move beyond a particular problem by generalizing to other situations:

3.1 Evaluate the reasonableness of the solution in the context of the original situation.

3.2 Note the method of deriving the solution and demonstrate a conceptual understanding of the derivation by solving similar problems.

3.3 Develop generalizations of the results obtained and apply them in other circumstances.

Math
2.1

Mathematical Reasoning

Estimating

Example:

Which of these should you use to
estimate 83 − 38 to the nearest ten?

(A)   80 − 30

(B)   80 − 40

(C)   90 − 40

(D)   90 − 30

Answer: (B)

Clue   Look carefully to see if you are rounding to the nearest 10 or to the
nearest 100.

DIRECTIONS: Choose the best answer.

1. Which number sentence would you use to
   estimate 97 × 9 to the nearest 100?

   (A)   90 × 5

   (B)   100 × 10

   (C)   90 × 10

   (D)   100 × 5

2. Which number sentence would you use to
   estimate 356 ÷ 192 to the nearest 100?

   (F)   350 ÷ 190

   (G)   300 ÷ 200

   (H)   400 ÷ 200

   (J)   400 ÷ 190

3. Estimate the answer to this problem by
   rounding.

   12 × 78

   (A)   700

   (B)   800

   (C)   600

   (D)   500

4. Shandra bought 19 pieces of candy to
   share with her friends. Each piece of
   candy cost 14 cents. Estimate how much
   she spent.

   (F) $.50

   (G) $1.00

   (H) $2.00

   (J) $ 2.50

5. Jason has $15.00. He wants to buy three
   things at the store:

   a new book for $7.88

   a new pen for $1.98

   a new bookmark for $1.33

   Use rounding to estimate how much
   money he will have left over.

   (A)   about $1.00

   (B)   about $2.00

   (C)   about $3.00

   (D)   about $4.00

STOP

Solving Complex Problems

 Clue Review the table carefully before moving on to the questions.

DIRECTIONS: Janna's favorite cereal cost $3.00 when she was 6 years old. It cost $3.50 when she was 8 years old, $4.00 when she was 9, and $4.50 when she was 10. Use the table to answer the questions.

Price of Cereal	
Year	**Cost**
1	$3.00
2	$3.50
3	$4.00
4	$4.50

1. In what year was the price the lowest?

- (A) 1
- (B) 2
- (C) 3
- (D) 4

2. How much did the price of cereal change over 4 years?

- (F) $.50
- (G) $1.00
- (H) $1.50
- (J) $2.00

3. What happened to the price of cereal between year 1 and year 4?

- (A) it doubled
- (B) it went up
- (C) it stayed the same
- (D) it went down

4. Predict what you think a box of cereal will cost in year 5.

- (F) $5.50
- (G) $3.00
- (H) $4.50
- (J) $5.00

5. Which graph correctly shows the change in price of Janna's cereal?

- (A)

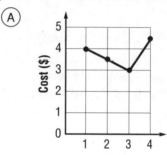

- (B)

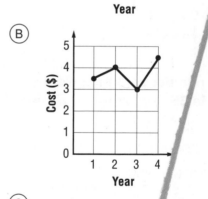

- (C)

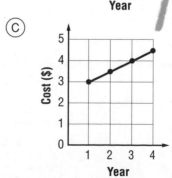

- (D) None of these

STOP

Name _____   Date _____

Using Mathematical Reasoning

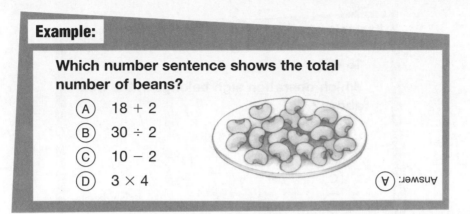

Example:

Which number sentence shows the total number of beans?

- (A) 18 + 2
- (B) 30 ÷ 2
- (C) 10 − 2
- (D) 3 × 4

Answer: (A)

Clue   Decide what useful information you can get from a picture, chart, or graph before you read the question.

1. **Look at the pattern of fruit. Which of these is the missing piece of fruit?**

- (A) orange
- (B) banana
- (C) pear
- (D) apple

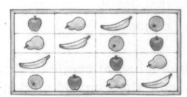

2. **Sarah just read that her town has the highest population in the county. Based on the chart below in which city does Sarah live?**

- (F) Kenton
- (G) Butler
- (H) Amity
- (J) Marion

Kenton	5,098
Butler	4,786
Amity	4,235
Marion	5,232

3. **Which animal is between 15 and 40 feet long?**

- (A) panda
- (B) sperm whale
- (C) Indian python
- (D) none of these

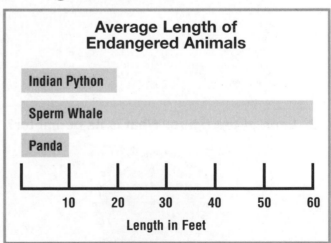

Average Length of Endangered Animals

Length in Feet

STOP

2.4

Understanding Math Terms

Example:

18 ■ 9 = 9

Which operation sign belongs in the box above?

(A) +

(B) −

(C) ×

(D) ÷

Answer: (B)

 Clue   When you are not sure of an answer, make your best guess and move on to the next problem.

DIRECTIONS: Choose the best answer.

1. 27 ■ 8 = 19   10 ■ 2 = 8

   Which operation sign belongs in both boxes above?

   (A) +

   (B) −

   (C) ×

   (D) ÷

2. **Look at the figure. What is its perimeter?**

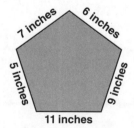

7 inches   6 inches
5 inches   9 inches
11 inches

   (F) 22 inches

   (G) 14 inches

   (H) 40 inches

   (J) 38 inches

3. **Tad wants to find the weight of a box of cereal. What unit of measurement will he probably find on the side of the box?**

   (A) millimeters

   (B) pounds

   (C) hectoliters

   (D) ounces

4. **You have a bag of candy to share with your class. There are 25 students in your class. You want each student to get 7 pieces. What operation will you need to use to figure out how many candies you need?**

   (F) addition

   (G) subtraction

   (H) multiplication

   (J) division

STOP

Math

2.5

Exact and Approximate Answers

Example:

Estimate the answer to each problem. Then use the space next to each problem to calculate the exact answer.

$$87 \times 5$$

Estimate   Exact answer   Difference between the two

_____   _____   _____

Answer: 450, 435, 15

---

1. Anna is selling wrapping paper to raise money for her school. Red paper is $1.35 a roll. Green paper is $1.79 a roll. Purple paper is $2.25 a roll. Anna sold 5 rolls of red paper, 2 rolls of green paper, and 1 roll of purple paper.

   _____ Estimate how much money she made.

   _____ Exactly how much money did she make?

   _____ What is the difference between your two answers?

2. Julio's brother is visiting his friend in Canada. It will take 3 days to make the drive. He drives 863 miles the first day, 412 miles the second day, and 942 miles the third day.

   _____ Estimate how many miles he drove in three days.

   _____ Exactly how many miles did he drive?

   _____ What is the difference between your two answers?

3. 33×6

   _____ Estimate

   _____ Exactly answer

   _____ Difference between the two

4. Three students in Alisha's school are collecting cans of food for the homeless. They collected 162 cans in all. Each student collected the same number of cans. How many did each student collect?

   _____ Estimate how many cans each student collected.

   _____ Exactly how many cans did each student collect?

   _____ What is the difference between your two answers?

STOP

Math

2.6

Analyzing a Math Problem

 Clue Look only for information that will help you solve the problem. Some information may not be useful.

DIRECTIONS: Read the story below, then answer the questions.

Cara and her father went to the grocery store. The closest store is 2 miles away. The store with the lowest prices is 5 miles away. The biggest store is 6 miles away. On the way to the store, her father stopped to buy gasoline. He bought 15 gallons of gas and paid $30.00. At the store, they bought 7 items:

1 pound of bananas
1 quart of milk
1 loaf of bread
2 dozen eggs
1 pound of butter
5 pounds of flour

The bill for the groceries was $9.82. Cara's father gave the cashier $10.00.

1. How much did one gallon of gas cost?

  (A) $1.00

  (B) $1.50

  (C) $2.00

  (D) $2.50

2. How much money did Cara's dad spend on their trip?

  (F) $40.00

  (G) $9.82

  (H) $20.18

  (J) $39.82

3. Cara's dad had $43.00 in his wallet. How much money did he have after the trip?

  (A) $15.00

  (B) $3.00

  (C) $3.18

  (D) $9.82

4. What would you need to know to find out if the groceries will fit in Cara's father's car?

  (F) the weight of the groceries

  (G) the cost of the groceries

  (H) the size of the groceries

  (J) the distance to the store

5. Cara wants to know how much time the trip will take. What is one thing she will need to know to find the answer?

  (A) the price of gas

  (B) the cost of groceries

  (C) the number of miles to the grocery store

  (D) the weight of the groceries

STOP

Mini-Test 2

DIRECTIONS: Look at the graph and then choose the best answer.

Average Daily Temperature

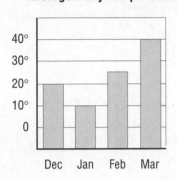

1. In which month was the temperature the lowest?

Ⓐ January

Ⓑ December

Ⓒ March

Ⓓ February

2. What was the average daily temperature in March?

Ⓕ 10°

Ⓖ 20°

Ⓗ 30°

Ⓙ 40°

3. How much did the average daily temperature change from February to March?

Ⓐ 25°

Ⓑ 15°

Ⓒ 10°

Ⓓ 5°

4. Sometimes you need exact information and sometimes you don't. Why would someone need to know the exact temperature?

Ⓕ to decide whether to wear a coat

Ⓖ to buy a thermometer

Ⓗ to bake a cake

Ⓙ to measure how much snow has fallen

5. Which of these line graphs show the same information as the temperature bar graph?

Ⓐ
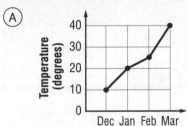

Ⓑ
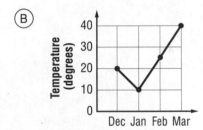

Ⓒ
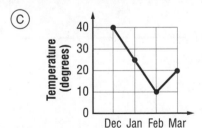

Ⓓ
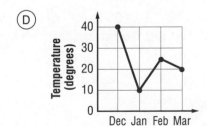

STOP

How Am I Doing?

Mini-Test 1 Page 153 **Number Correct**	**3** answers correct	**Great Job!** Move on to the section test on page 163.
	2 answers correct	**You're almost there!** But you still need a little practice. Review practice pages 151–152 before moving on to the section test on page 163.
	0–1 answers correct	**Oops!** Time to review what you have learned and try again. Review the practice section on pages 151–152. Then retake the test on page 153. Now move on to the section test on page 163.
Mini-Test 2 Page 161 **Number Correct**	**5** answers correct	**Awesome!** Move on to the section test on page 163.
	3–4 answers correct	**You're almost there!** But you still need a little practice. Review practice pages 155–160 before moving on to the section test on page 163.
	0–2 answers correct	**Oops!** Time to review what you have learned and try again. Review the practice section on pages 155–160. Then retake the test on page 161. Now move on to the section test on page 163.

Final Mathematical Reasoning Test
for pages 151–161

DIRECTIONS: Choose the best answer.

1. It takes Cassie $10\frac{1}{2}$ minutes to run a mile. She is 2 miles from home. It is 2:15 P.M. Cassie must be home for lunch at 2:30. When will she get there?

  Ⓐ 2:35
  Ⓑ 2:31
  Ⓒ 2:36
  Ⓓ 2:28

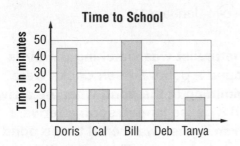

Time to School

This graph shows how long it takes students to ride the bus to school. Study the graph, then answer numbers 2 and 3.

2. Whose trip is less than half an hour?

  Ⓕ Deb and Tanya
  Ⓖ Doris and Bill
  Ⓗ Cal and Deb
  Ⓙ Cal and Tanya

3. If Bill's father drives him to school, he saves 15 minutes. How long does it take Bill to get to school if his father drives?

  Ⓐ 50 minutes
  Ⓑ 35 minutes
  Ⓒ 25 minutes
  Ⓓ 15 minutes

4. Mr. Miller sold 7 cars in 7 days. He sold the same number of cars each day. How many did he sell each day?

  Ⓕ 1
  Ⓖ 3
  Ⓗ 5
  Ⓙ 7

5. There are 48 chairs around the tables in the library. There are 8 chairs at each table. How many tables are in the library?

  Ⓐ 48
  Ⓑ 8
  Ⓒ 6
  Ⓓ 7

6. A piece of wire is 2 feet long. If you use 14 inches of the wire, how many inches are left?

  Ⓕ 9 inches
  Ⓖ 10 inches
  Ⓗ 11 inches
  Ⓙ 1 foot

7. A train has 850 seats. There are 317 empty seats. How many people are seated?

  Ⓐ 533
  Ⓑ 317
  Ⓒ 850
  Ⓓ 1,383

GO

One liter is a little more that 1 quart. Use that information to estimate how many liters each of these containers would hold.

8.
- (F) 1 liter
- (G) 8 liters
- (H) 12 liters
- (J) 45 liters

9.
- (A) 25 liters
- (B) 18 liters
- (C) 9 liters
- (D) 2 liters

10.
- (F) 20 liters
- (G) 4 liters
- (H) 2 liters
- (J) 1 liter

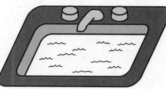

Use this calendar to answer questions 11 through 13.

January						
SUN	MON	TUE	WED	THU	FRI	SAT
1	2	3	4	5	6	7
8	9	10	11	12	13	14
15	16	17	18	19	20	21
22	23	24	25	26	27	28
29	30	31				

11. This calendar is for January. What day of the week was the last day in December?
- (A) Monday
- (B) Saturday
- (C) Sunday
- (D) Tuesday

12. How many Tuesdays are in January?
- (F) 3
- (G) 4
- (H) 5
- (J) 6

13. For the class trip this year, the students are going on a camping trip. The trip will begin on the third Wednesday in January and ending the following Saturday. What date will the camping trip begin?
- (A) January 4
- (B) January 25
- (C) January 21
- (D) January 18

14. A naturalist was watching the birds around a pond. Fifteen ducks were swimming in the pond when he arrived, and 8 geese landed soon afterward. Seven cranes wandered to the pond from a nearby swamp. They were followed by 3 turtles. How many birds in all did the naturalist see?
- (F) 30
- (G) 29
- (H) 19
- (J) 5

15. Five children were having pizza for dinner. Michael had 2 slices, Colby had 1 slice, Stacey had 3 slices, and Jorge had 2 slices. How many slices did Mark have?
- (A) 1 slice
- (B) 3 slices
- (C) 2 slices
- (D) not enough information

GO

16. Miss Cohen teaches piano lessons to 7 students every day. Each lesson lasts 30 minutes. How long does Miss Cohen teach each day?

    (F) 3 hours

    (G) 3 hours 30 minutes

    (H) 7 hours

    (J) not enough information

Use the graph to answer questions 17 through 19.

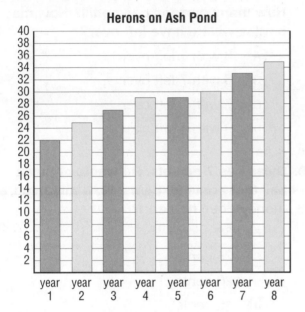

Herons on Ash Pond

17. In which two years did the number of herons stay the same?

    (A) years 1 and 2

    (B) years 2 and 3

    (C) years 3 and 4

    (D) years 4 and 5

18. How many more herons were there in year 8 than in year 1?

    (F) 10

    (G) 11

    (H) 13

    (J) 14

19. Using the information on the graph, what could you predict for year 11?

    (A) The number of herons will increase.

    (B) The number of herons will decrease.

    (C) The number of herons will stay the same.

    (D) Herons will become endangered species.

20. Which number sentence would you use to estimate 448 ÷ 212 to the nearest 100?

    (F) 450 ÷ 210

    (G) 440 ÷ 210

    (H) 500 ÷ 200

    (J) 400 ÷ 200

21. Estimate the answer to this problem by rounding.

    56 × 12

    (A) 500

    (B) 600

    (C) 560

    (D) 1,000

22. Which of these should you use to estimate 44 − 19 to the nearest 10?

    (F) 40 − 20

    (G) 45 − 15

    (H) 50 − 20

    (J) 40 − 10

23. Which of these would you probably measure in meters?

    (A) the height of a tree

    (B) the distance between two cities

    (C) the weight of a horse

    (D) the amount of medicine in a bottle

GO

24. A number rounded to the nearest 10 is 550. When it is rounded to the nearest 100, the number becomes 600. Which of these numbers could it be?

(F) 554

(G) 545

(H) 559

(J) 549

25. The roller coaster at the local fair is 27 feet high. The roller coaster at the amusement park is 12 times taller that that. Estimate the height of the roller coaster at the amusement park.

(A) 270 feet

(B) 300 feet

(C) 400 feet

(D) 200 feet

26. A large school bus can carry 98 students. Estimate how many students it can carry on 8 trips.

(F) 720

(G) 800

(H) 900

(J) 950

27. Mrs. Compton spent $15 on groceries on Monday, $29 on Wednesday, and $67 on Saturday. Estimate the total amount of money she spent on groceries.

(A) $110

(B) $120

(C) $100

(D) $125

28. A plane flies 900 kilometers in 2 hours. It flies the same distance each hour. How far does the plane travel each hour?

(F) 450 miles

(G) 500 miles

(H) 350 miles

(J) 400 miles

29. Sam has 63 empty bottles. He wants to put them into cartons of 8 bottles each. How many cartons can he fill? How may bottles will he have left over?

(A) 8 with 1 left over

(B) 8 with 7 left over

(C) 7 with 7 left over

(D) 9 with 1 left over

30. Dylan has 7 nickels. He wants to buy a ball that costs 60 cents. How much more money does he need?

(F) 30 cents

(G) 25 cents

(H) 20 cents

(J) 15 cents

STOP

Name _____   Date _____

Mathematical Reasoning Test
Answer Sheet

1	Ⓐ Ⓑ Ⓒ Ⓓ	21	Ⓐ Ⓑ Ⓒ Ⓓ
2	Ⓕ Ⓖ Ⓗ Ⓙ	22	Ⓕ Ⓖ Ⓗ Ⓙ
3	Ⓐ Ⓑ Ⓒ Ⓓ	23	Ⓐ Ⓑ Ⓒ Ⓓ
4	Ⓕ Ⓖ Ⓗ Ⓙ	24	Ⓕ Ⓖ Ⓗ Ⓙ
5	Ⓐ Ⓑ Ⓒ Ⓓ	25	Ⓐ Ⓑ Ⓒ Ⓓ
6	Ⓕ Ⓖ Ⓗ Ⓙ	26	Ⓕ Ⓖ Ⓗ Ⓙ
7	Ⓐ Ⓑ Ⓒ Ⓓ	27	Ⓐ Ⓑ Ⓒ Ⓓ
8	Ⓕ Ⓖ Ⓗ Ⓙ	28	Ⓕ Ⓖ Ⓗ Ⓙ
9	Ⓐ Ⓑ Ⓒ Ⓓ	29	Ⓐ Ⓑ Ⓒ Ⓓ
10	Ⓕ Ⓖ Ⓗ Ⓙ	30	Ⓕ Ⓖ Ⓗ Ⓙ

11	Ⓐ Ⓑ Ⓒ Ⓓ
12	Ⓕ Ⓖ Ⓗ Ⓙ
13	Ⓐ Ⓑ Ⓒ Ⓓ
14	Ⓕ Ⓖ Ⓗ Ⓙ
15	Ⓐ Ⓑ Ⓒ Ⓓ
16	Ⓕ Ⓖ Ⓗ Ⓙ
17	Ⓐ Ⓑ Ⓒ Ⓓ
18	Ⓕ Ⓖ Ⓗ Ⓙ
19	Ⓐ Ⓑ Ⓒ Ⓓ
20	Ⓕ Ⓖ Ⓗ Ⓙ

Answer Key

Page 8
1. A
2. G
3. C
4. J

Page 9
1. B
2. J
3. B
4. H
5. A
6. G

Page 10
1. A
2. S
3. S
4. S
5. A
6. A
7. A
8. S
9. S
10. S
11. A
12. S

Page 11
1. B
2. F
3. D
4. H
5. B

Page 12
1. C
2. J
3. A

Page 13
1. B
2. G
3. A
4. J
5. A

Page 14
1. D
2. J
3. A
4. G
5. C
6. G
7. D

Page 15 Mini-Test
1. C
2. F
3. B
4. J
5. A
6. J
7. C
8. F
9. B

Page 17
1. A
2. H
3. B
4. J
5. A
6. F

Page 18
1. C
2. 2, 4, 3, 1
3. F
4. Sentences should describe how seeds are transported from one place to another.

Page 19
1. B
2. J
3. A

Page 20
1. sunset
2. beach
3. Gabe, Hannah
4. He finds a horseshoe crab and needs to know if it will hurt him.
5. Answers will vary but students should recognize that Gabe will make an effort to find out more about horseshoe crabs to reassure himself that they are not harmful. Students should underline the following quote: "I want to know more about them."

Page 21
located: in Pacific Ocean near equator; 650 miles west of Ecuador
famous for: pirates once buried treasure there; unusual animals and birds

Page 22
1. No. Coupons are only available on the first day of the sale—August 1.
2. No. He would have to buy a pair of shoes that cost at least $20 to get free socks.
3. No. The special is not good at the Lakewood store.
4. The socks must cost less than $2.00 a pair.

Page 23
1. A
2. false
3. Step #3

Page 24 Mini-Test
1. D
2. H
3. B
4. G

Page 26
1. B
2. Squirrels can't talk in real life. The passage tells a story.
3. Fiction is usually a story about something that did not really happen. Fiction includes details about a made-up place and events.

Page 27
1. A
2. G
3. D
4. J

Page 28
1. **A.** Dylan
   B. Danny
   C. Danny
   D. Dylan
2. Dylan's day
3. Students should tell whether their reaction would be most like Dylan's or Danny's.

Page 29
1. A
2. The author said that he or she is sad when whales beach themselves.
3. J

Page 30
1. D
2. G
3. A
4. G
5. D
6. H
7. C

Page 31
1. Samantha. Her birthday
2. Samantha's mother. She says "her father and me."
3. Her sister. She was mentioned in Section A. She talks about her mom and dad.

Page 32 Mini-Test
1. C
2. G
3. C
4. G
5. B
6. H

Page 34–37 Final Reading Test
1. D
2. H
3. A
4. J
5. C
6. H
7. A
8. J
9. B
10. G
11. C
12. J
13. D
14. G
15. C
16. G
17. B
18. G
19. B
20. G
21. C
22. F
23. D
24. H
25. C
26. H

Page 40
Many insects find a warm place to spend the winter. Ants dig deep in the ground. Beetles stack up under rocks or dead leaves. Bees gather in a ball in their hive.

Page 41
1. A
2. H
3. B
4. J
5. C
6. G
7. C
8. F

Page 42
1. A
2. J
3. B
4. G
5. B
6. H

Page 43 Mini-Test
1. B
2. H
3. D
4. F
5. A
6. F

Page 45
1. Students should describe their main character.
2. Students should describe where and when their story takes place.
3. Students should present the main problem that will be introduced in their story and how it will be resolved by their main character.

Page 46
1. Students should describe their favorite class.
2. Students should give details about why they consider one class to be their favorite.
3. Students should provide at least one suggestion of how their favorite class could be improved.

Page 47
Letters should explain why the student should be allowed to do something of his or her choosing. Students should construct their letters with an appropriate greeting and closing and use correct punctuation and spelling.

Page 48 Mini-Test
1. Students' sentences should include sensory language to describe how something looks, feels, smells, or tastes.
2. Students should write a thank-you note to someone who has given them a gift or done something special for them. Letters should include a proper greeting and closing and correct punctuation and spelling.

Pages 50–53 Final Writing Test
1. A
2. H
3. C
4. G
5. A
6. A
7. H
8. D
9. H
10. A
11. B
12. F
13. C
14. F
15. B
16. J
17. D
18. F
19. A
20. J
21. C
22. G

Page 57
1. A
2. H
3. C
4. J
5. B
6. G
7. A
8. F
9. H

Page 58
1. D
2. H
3. B
4. G
5. C
6. J
7. A
8. H
9. C

Page 59
1. B
2. J
3. B
4. F
5. B
6. H

Page 60
1. B
2. J
3. C
4. G
5. A
6. F

Page 61
1. A
2. H
3. A
4. J
5. A
6. H
7. A

Page 62
1. D
2. H
3. D
4. H
5. C
6. J
7. C

Page 63
1. D
2. H
3. A
4. H
5. D
6. H
7. C

Page 64
1. B
2. J
3. C
4. H
5. D
6. F
7. D
8. H
9. C

Page 65
1. C
2. F
3. C
4. H
5. A
6. J
7. A
8. F

Page 66 Mini-Test
1. D
2. J
3. C
4. H
5. C
6. H
7. B
8. H
9. D
10. H

Pages 68–71 Final Language Conventions Test
1. D
2. F
3. C
4. F
5. B
6. H
7. C
8. G
9. D
10. J
11. A
12. J
13. C
14. G
15. B
16. G
17. B
18. H
19. D
20. H
21. C
22. J
23. B
24. H
25. D
26. H
27. A
28. J
29. B
30. F
31. B
32. J
33. C
34. G
35. D
36. J
37. C
38. H
39. B
40. H
41. D

Page 75
1. C
2. G
3. D
4. G
5. B
6. H
7. C

Page 76
1. C
2. G
3. B
4. G
5. A
6. G
7. C
8. G

Page 77
1. A
2. J
3. C
4. G
5. C

Page 78
1. 900, 700, 900
   500, 200, 400
   400, 500, 200
2. 2,000; 3,000;
   4,000
   7,000; 9,000;
   6,000
   5,000; 9,000;
   3,000
3. B
4. J
5. A
6. G

Page 79
1. B
2. J
3. D
4. G
5. B
6. J
7. D
8. F

Page 80 Mini-Test
1. A
2. H
3. B
4. H
5. A
6. J
7. C
8. H

Page 82
1. D
2. G
3. C
4. F
5. D
6. H
7. D
8. J

Page 83
1. B
2. F
3. A
4. H
5. D
6. H
7. B
8. H
9. A
10. G

Page 84
1. Example
2. $3\overline{)177}$
3. $3\overline{)63}$
4. $3\overline{)126}$
5. $3\overline{)54}$
6. $3\overline{)30}$
7. $3\overline{)174}$
8. $3\overline{)84}$
9. $3\overline{)234}$
10. $3\overline{)246}$

Page 85
1. A
2. H
3. B
4. F
5. C
6. J
7. A
8. F

Page 86
1. A
2. H
3. C
4. F
5. B
6. J
7. A
8. J
9. B
10. F

Page 87
1. Rule 3
2. Rule 2
3. Rule 1
4. Rule 4
5. Rule 2
6. Rule 1
7. Rule 3
8. Rule 2

Page 88
1. B
2. H
3. C
4. H

Page 89
1. A
2. J
3. D
4. J
5. D
6. H
7. A
8. H

Page 90 Mini-Test
1. B
2. H
3. A
4. J
5. C
6. F
7. B
8. H
9. B

Page 92
1. B
2. J
3. D
4. J
5. B

Page 93
1. D
2. H
3. B
4. H
5. A
6. G
7. C

Page 94
1. B
2. F
3. C
4. H
5. C
6. F
7. D
8. G
9. B

Page 95
1. D
2. F
3. C
4. H
5. C
6. F

Page 96 Mini-Test
1. B
2. F
3. C
4. H
5. A
6. J
7. D
8. J

Pages 98–101 Final Number Sense Test
1. C
2. F
3. A
4. H
5. C
6. J
7. B
8. J
9. B
10. G
11. D
12. H
13. D
14. H
15. C
16. G
17. C
18. G
19. C
20. H
21. C
22. H
23. D
24. H
25. C
26. G
27. A
28. F
29. D
30. F
31. C
32. J
33. C
34. F
35. A
36. F
37. C

Page 104
1. A
2. F
3. D
4. G
5. D
6. J

Page 105
1. B
2. H
3. A
4. H
5. B
6. H
7. D

Page 106
1. C
2. J
3. B
4. G
5. D
6. J
7. A

Page 107
1. B
2. F
3. D
4. H
5. C
6. H

Page 108
1. A
2. G
3. C
4. H
5. C
6. H

Page 109 Mini-Test
1. B
2. J
3. C
4. H
5. A
6. J
7. C
8. G
9. B
10. H

Page 111
1. B
2. J
3. C
4. G
5. C
6. G

Page 112
1. D
2. H
3. C
4. J
5. D
6. F

Page 113 Mini-Test
1. C
2. J
3. D
4. F
5. C
6. J
7. B

Pages 115-118 Final Algebra and Functions Test
1. A
2. H
3. B
4. G
5. A
6. J
7. C
8. G
9. C
10. F
11. A
12. G
13. B
14. F
15. D
16. F
17. D
18. H
19. D
20. J
21. B
22. F
23. D
24. H
25. B
26. G
27. C
28. J
29. C
30. J
31. B
32. G
33. C
34. J
35. C
36. F
37. D
38. H
39. D

Page 121
1. C
2. J
3. B

Page 122
1. 5
2. 6
3. 6
4. 5,5
5. 8,8
6. 12,12

Page 123
1. 12 cm
2. 36 in.
3. 89 ft.
4. 77 m
5. 65 km
6. 22 in.
7. 84 mm
8. 72 yds.
9. 33 m

Page 124
1. B
2. F
3. C
4. H
5. B
6. J

Page 125 Mini-Test
1. C
2. J
3. B
4. H
5. C
6. J
7. A

Page 127
1. C
2. H
3. C
4. G
5. A
6. G

Page 128
1. B
2. F
3. B
4. H
5. A
6. G

Page 129
1. B
2. J
3. A
4. G
5. D

Page 130
1. B
2. F
3. A
4. H
5. B
6. H

Page 131
1. C
2. J
3. C
4. F
5. C
6. G

Page 132
1. B
2. F
3. D
4. H
5. D
6. F
7. D
8. F

Page 133 Mini-Test
1. C
2. G
3. C
4. H
5. D
6. G

Pages 135–138
Final Measurement
and Geometry Test
1. C
2. F
3. C
4. H
5. C
6. H
7. A
8. F
9. C
10. H
11. D
12. G
13. B
14. G
15. A
16. H
17. A
18. J
19. B
20. J
21. D

Page 141
1. A
2. J
3. B
4. H
5. C
6. J
7. A

Page 142
1. C
2. H
3. D
4. G
5. A
6. G

Page 143
1. C
2. G
3. A
4. H
5. D

Page 144
1. C
2. H
3. B
4. H

Page 145 Mini-Test
1. D
2. G
3. A
4. G
5. D
6. G
7. D
8. F
9. C

Pages 147–148
Final Statistics,
Data Analysis, and
Probability Test
1. A
2. J
3. C
4. H
5. A
6. G
7. C
8. J
9. D
10. F
11. A
12. G
13. D

Page 151
1. C
2. F
3. A
4. H
5. D

Page 152
1. B
2. G
3. C
4. G
5. D

Page 153 Mini-Test
1. A
2. G
3. D

Page 155
1. B
2. H
3. B
4. H
5. D

Page 156
1. A
2. H
3. B
4. J
5. C

Page 157
1. A
2. J
3. C

Page 158
1. B
2. J
3. D
4. H

Page 159
1. $11; $12.58; $1.58
2. 2,200 miles; 2,217 miles; 17 miles
3. 180, 198, 18
4. 66, 54, 12

Page 160
1. C
2. J
3. C
4. H
5. C

Page 161 Mini-Test
1. A
2. J
3. B
4. H
5. B

Pages 163–166 Final
Mathematical
Reasoning Test
1. C
2. J
3. B
4. F
5. C
6. G
7. A
8. F
9. D
10. F
11. B
12. H
13. D
14. F
15. D
16. G
17. D
18. H
19. A
20. J
21. B
22. F
23. A
24. F
25. B
26. G
27. B
28. F
29. C
30. G